THE COUNCIL OF FIFTY

THE COUNCIL OF FIFTY

What the Records Reveal about Mormon History

MATTHEW J. GROW & R. ERIC SMITH

Editors

RSC
BYU

DESERET
BOOK

Published by the Religious Studies Center, Brigham Young University, Provo, Utah, in cooperation with Deseret Book Company, Salt Lake City.

Visit us at rsc.byu.edu.

Printed in the United States of America by Sheridan Books, Inc.

DESERET BOOK is a registered trademark of Deseret Book Company.

Visit us at DeseretBook.com.

Cover design and interior layout by Madison Swapp.

ISBN: 978-1-9443-9421-9
Retail US: $21.99

Library of Congress Cataloging-in-Publication Data

Names: Grow, Matthew J., editor.
Title: The Council of Fifty : what the records reveal about Mormon history / edited
    by Matthew J. Grow and R. Eric Smith.
Description: Provo : Religious Studies Center BYU, 2017. | Includes index.
Identifiers: LCCN 2017017269 | ISBN 9781944394219
Subjects: LCSH: Council of Fifty (Church of Jesus Christ of Latter-day Saints)--
    History--Sources. | Church of Jesus Christ of Latter-day Saints--History--19th
    century. | Mormon Church--History--19th century.
Classification: LCC BX8611 .C6654 2017 | DDC 289.309/034--dc23 LC record
    available at https://lccn.loc.gov/2017017269

CONTENTS

INTRODUCTION

Before he traveled to Carthage, Illinois, in late June 1844 to surrender on an arrest warrant, Joseph Smith called William Clayton, a trusted clerk, to his side. Less than three months earlier, Joseph Smith had formed a confidential council consisting of roughly fifty men. The council, which became known as the "Council of Fifty" or "Kingdom of God," was to "look to some place where we can go and establish a Theocracy either in Texas or Oregon or somewhere in California." Furthermore, Joseph Smith had told them, the council "was designed to be got up for the safety and salvation of the saints by protecting them in their religious rights and worship."[1] The members of the council believed that it would protect the political and temporal interests of the Church in anticipation of the return of Jesus Christ and his millennial reign.

Now, shortly before going to Carthage, he instructed Clayton to destroy or hide the records of the council. Joseph Smith feared that the candid discussions within the Council of Fifty—including the desire to establish a theocracy—could be used against him in either a court of law or, more likely, the court of public opinion. Clayton opted to bury the records in his garden.

A few days after Joseph Smith was killed by a mob in Carthage, Clayton dug up the records of the Council of Fifty. He then copied the minutes of the council's meetings into more permanent record books and continued taking minutes after Brigham Young reassembled the Council of Fifty in February 1845. Over the next year, the council met to discuss how to govern the city of Nauvoo after the state of Illinois revoked its municipal charter and how to find a settlement place for the Latter-day Saints in the West. The council's final meetings in Nauvoo occurred in the partially completed Nauvoo Temple in January 1846, just a few weeks before the Saints began to cross the frozen Mississippi on their way west.

As they headed west, Church leaders took the minutes of the council meetings with them. The council met for periods of time in Utah Territory under Brigham Young and then under his successor, John Taylor. At some point, the records of the council became part of the archives of the Church's First Presidency.

Historians have long known of the existence of the council and the minutes of its meetings. Until recently, though, the minutes had never been made available for historical research. Because of their inaccessibility— and because historians knew that they were made during a critical and controversial era of Mormon history—a mystique grew up surrounding the minutes. What did they contain? Why had they been withheld? Some speculated that the council's minutes must contain explosive details about the final months of Joseph Smith's life or the initial era of Brigham Young's leadership of the Church. Indeed, the minutes had become a sort of "holy grail" of early Mormon documents.

Other records regarding the council's activities are likewise scarce. Members of the council took an oath of confidentiality when they joined, meaning that many members left no records that discussed the council. Nevertheless, some members later spoke about the council publicly and others left private records in journals and letters. Over the past several decades, these additional records have allowed several scholars—especially Klaus J. Hansen, D. Michael Quinn, Andrew F. Ehat, and Jedediah S. Rogers—to gain an understanding of the Council of Fifty. While they each made important contributions, lack of access to the core minutes meant that their scholarship remained tentative, as each recognized.[2]

Since the beginning of the Joseph Smith Papers Project in the early 2000s, project leaders have emphasized that the papers will contain a comprehensive edition of all of Smith's papers, published in print, online, or both. Many outside the project initially wondered if that would include documents that had previously not been made accessible to scholars. The first major indication that the edition would truly be comprehensive was the publication of one of Joseph Smith's manuscript revelation books, called the Book of Commandments and Revelations, that had been part of the collection of the Church's First Presidency and had never before been made available.[3] Still, historians questioned whether the project would ever publish the minutes of the Council of Fifty.

The minutes had never been previously available for at least two key reasons: first, because they were considered confidential during the council's meetings, and later stewards of the records wished to honor that confidentiality; and second, because once they were in the possession of the First Presidency, they were seldom used or read by Church leaders, and there was no pressing reason to make them available. The Church's commitment to publish all of Joseph Smith's documents as part of *The Joseph Smith Papers* provided the appropriate moment for their release.

We had the privilege of being involved with preparing the minutes for publication. In fall 2012, Matthew J. Grow was asked by Reid L. Neilson, managing director of the Church History Department, to study a transcript of the Council of Fifty minutes and—with the assistance of Ronald K. Esplin, a general editor of the Joseph Smith Papers—to write an introduction to the minutes that would help inform Church leaders regarding their contents.

Several months later, we learned that the First Presidency had granted permission to use the council's minutes in the publication of Joseph Smith's final journals (the third volume of the Journals series of *The Joseph Smith Papers*). This volume was nearly complete, but we had put publication on hold pending this decision because the journal refers to the Council of Fifty and we hoped to use insights from the minutes in our annotation. Significantly, the First Presidency also granted permission to publish the council's minutes as a separate volume in *The Joseph Smith Papers*.

After project leaders learned this news, they assembled a meeting of the staff of the Joseph Smith Papers Project on May 1, 2013. At the meeting, Elder Steven E. Snow, Church Historian and Recorder, announced the decision to the jubilation of the staff. We were then allowed to see and hold the three small record books that contained the council's minutes in the

These three small record books contain William Clayton's minutes of the Nauvoo Council of Fifty. Photograph by Welden C. Andersen. Courtesy of Church History Library, Salt Lake City.

distinctive handwriting of William Clayton. As historians and editors who had long studied the Council of Fifty and hoped that the minutes would be included in *The Joseph Smith Papers*, this was a remarkable meeting. Eric Smith recorded in his journal that evening, "This is a day long anticipated by Mormon historians: the opportunity to publish these minutes, which the world has known about for a long time and which critics of the Church have often conjectured contain material that will embarrass the Church. I feel privileged to be involved with this project and to be one of the few people who has seen these minutes."

We were asked to keep the decision confidential until a public announcement was made. Notwithstanding our collective excitement, we honored the request not to talk about the prospective publication of the minutes until Elder Snow made a public announcement in an interview with the *Church News* in September 2013.[4] Following the public announcement, we could talk more freely about our work on the minutes.

After the permission came, we quickly assembled a team of historians, led by Grow. Ronald K. Esplin brought his deep knowledge about both Joseph Smith and Brigham Young to the task. Mark Ashurst-McGee, who had written a dissertation on early Mormon political thought, added perspective on those issues and did the final textual verification. Gerrit J. Dirkmaat's dissertation had likewise probed a relevant topic: the relationship between the Mormons and the United States between 1844 and 1854. Finally, Jeffrey D. Mahas brought his indefatigable research skills and archival sensibilities to the task. Most of us were working on other projects simultaneously with the Council of Fifty minutes, but all of us were thrilled to have a part in writing the introductions and footnotes that would be published along with the minutes. Historians generally love working with documents that haven't been used much by scholars previously. But the council minutes were something else entirely: a document not only made newly available, but one that had been the subject of tremendous speculation and contained critical information on early Mormon thought and governance.

The volume editors listed on the cover page were, however, only a small part of the team at the Joseph Smith Papers Project who assisted with the publication of the minutes. Eric Smith led the editorial team that helped transcribe the minutes and verify their text, meticulously checked the thousands of sources used in the annotation, edited and then edited and edited again the introductions and footnotes, selected images, performed genealogical research, designed maps, and helped promote the book. Among the roughly two dozen individuals who assisted with such work were Rachel Osborne, source checker; Shannon Kelly, editor; Kay Darowski and Joseph F. Darowski, text verifiers; Jeffrey G. Cannon, photoarchivist; Ed Brinton and Alison Palmer, typesetters; and Kate Mertes, indexer.

As we began talking about the council's minutes publicly in anticipation of their 2016 publication, we learned that notwithstanding the mystique the Council of Fifty had gained among the historical community and the importance of the council to early Latter-day Saints, the organization itself is little known among modern Latter-day Saints. The Mormon tendency to use numbers to name quorums and councils did not help matters. "Do you mean the Council of *Seventy*?" many wondered. The lack of knowledge is not particularly surprising; while a few scattered references to the Council of Fifty have appeared in the Church's magazines in the past several decades, the council has not received much other official attention from the Church.[5] For instance, the Church's study manual *Teachings of Presidents of the Church: Joseph Smith* does not contain any references to the council.

While the council's minutes are very readable—containing as they do relatively complete records of discussions, debates, and decisions—we knew that most individuals interested in Mormon history and theology would simply not have the time or inclination to wade through the nearly eight hundred pages in the published *Joseph Smith Papers* volume to gain an understanding of the Council of Fifty.

In addition, we were convinced that the council's minutes needed to be engaged by scholars to evaluate the question of how these minutes should change our collective understanding of the Latter-day Saint past. The minutes speak on a broad range of fascinating issues—Mormon thought on earthly and heavenly constitutions and government, Joseph Smith's presidential campaign, the murder of Joseph and Hyrum Smith, Mormon relationships with American Indians, the transition to the leadership of Brigham Young, the response to the revocation of the Nauvoo charter, the completion of the Nauvoo Temple, dissent and vigilante violence in and around Nauvoo, Latter-day Saint thought on religious liberty, and the planning for the exodus west.

Furthermore, the minutes illuminate a crucial era in the Mormon past that has not received adequate attention from historians. Often, histories underemphasize the critical era between the two events often used as a shorthand to define this time period: the Martyrdom and the Trek West. The era between March 1844 and January 1846—or, roughly, between Joseph Smith's murder and the Mormon exodus from Illinois—is a particularly important time of transition in Mormon history. The council's minutes allow us an unprecedented window into the thinking of Latter-day Saints during this era, including their grand ambitions to establish the kingdom of God and fulfill prophecies from the Bible and Book of Mormon, their devastation at the murders of Joseph and Hyrum Smith, their alienation and anger at the United States because of these murders and other persecution, and their determination to find a place of safety and refuge in western North America where they could build their kingdom in peace.

The minutes of the Council of Fifty shape historical understanding not just of Mormon history but of larger events in US and international history. In the council's deliberations—including over Joseph Smith's presidential campaign and the past treatment of the Latter-day Saints—Smith and other members highlighted their views of the failure of the US Constitution and of federal, state, and local governments to adequately protect religious liberty. Under the government system of that time, the constitutional protections of religious liberty did not yet apply to state and local governments, and the Mormons believed that the tyranny of the majority had imperiled their liberty. In addition, the council's minutes demonstrate the Mormons' desire to potentially settle outside of the United States, as they explored the independent Republic of Texas, California (then a part of Mexico), and Oregon (then disputed between Great Britain and the United States) as possible settlement sites. Mormons thus presented the US government with a geopolitical challenge, as they sought to establish settlements beyond the boundaries of the United States.

We asked each of the scholars in this volume to consider a question: How do the Council of Fifty minutes change our understanding of Mormon history? In other words, why do they matter? Three of the papers in this volume began as initial scholarly reactions—before the Council of Fifty minutes were published—at the Mormon History Association's annual conference in June

2016. Two additional essays were presented at a conference at the University of Virginia at the launch of the publication of the minutes in September 2016. All of the essays are published here for the first time.

This volume opens with an essay by preeminent historian Richard Lyman Bushman, professor emeritus from Columbia University and biographer of Joseph Smith, who considers the broad ramifications of the minutes for Mormon history. Richard E. Turley Jr., who played a role in obtaining permission to publish the minutes during his time as Assistant Church Historian and Recorder of The Church of Jesus Christ of Latter-day Saints, examines one key context for the establishment of the council: violence against the Latter-day Saints, particularly in Missouri in the 1830s.

Several essays examine the three months that the council met under Joseph Smith in early 1844. Spencer W. McBride, an early American historian who works for the Joseph Smith Papers Project, demonstrates how the minutes shed new light on Joseph Smith's campaign for the US presidency. The minutes also illustrate Joseph Smith's thinking on the blending of theocracy and democracy, captured with the evocative term "theodemocracy," as explored in the essay by Patrick Q. Mason, Howard W. Hunter Chair of Mormon Studies at Claremont Graduate University. Benjamin E. Park, an assistant professor of history at Sam Houston State University, places the questions raised by the council in broader American political thinking. The essay by Nathan B. Oman, professor of law at William & Mary Law School, likewise contextualizes the council's attempt to write a constitution in the milieu of US political thought and constitution-writing in the nineteenth century.

The next two essays look at the minutes broadly. Gerrit J. Dirkmaat, an assistant professor of Church history and doctrine at Brigham Young University, highlights some of the most important statements in the minutes by Joseph Smith, Brigham Young, and other Church leaders on topics ranging from religious liberty to friendship to how councils should operate. R. Eric Smith explores insights that the Council of Fifty minutes provide into broader Mormon record-keeping practices of that period.

The essays then transition to examine the council as it operated under Brigham Young from February 1845 to January 1846. The essay by Matthew J. Grow and Marilyn Bradford assesses what the Council of

Fifty minutes demonstrate about Brigham Young's personality, leadership style, and priorities as leader of the Latter-day Saints. Jeffrey D. Mahas, a documentary editor at the Joseph Smith Papers Project, examines one of the council's key objectives: encouraging conversion of and exploring alliances with American Indians. As Matthew C. Godfrey, managing historian of *The Joseph Smith Papers*, discusses in his essay, the council took several steps to complete the Nauvoo House, a large boardinghouse in Nauvoo that the Saints had been commanded to build in a revelation to Joseph Smith.

Two essays then consider the role of the council in planning for the Saints' exodus from Nauvoo. Disputes over where the Mormons should ultimately settle led to divisions within the Quorum of the Twelve and the Church, as Christopher James Blythe, a historian with the Joseph Smith Papers Project, discusses in his essay on apostle Lyman Wight. Richard E. Bennett, a leading expert on the Mormon exodus and professor of Church history and doctrine at Brigham Young University, then examines how the council's minutes both confirm existing scholarship on the exodus and add new light.

The final two essays examine broad themes in the council's history, particularly in the context of western US history. Jedediah S. Rogers, co-managing editor of the *Utah Historical Quarterly* and author of a book on the Council of Fifty that focuses on the Utah period, places the council in the context of history writing about the American West. In his concluding essay, W. Paul Reeve, professor of history at the University of Utah, reflects on the contributions of the minutes, including in highlighting the Mormons' search for religious liberty in the West.[6]

As demonstrated by these essays, the Council of Fifty minutes provide crucial insights into Latter-day Saint history in these critical years. While historians already knew the broad outlines of much of what was discussed in the council, the minutes provide tremendous detail on the discussions and deliberations that led to the actions taken by Joseph Smith, Brigham Young, and other Mormon leaders during this time.

We hope that this collection of essays both increases public knowledge about the Council of Fifty and spurs future scholarship. Dissertations, articles, and books remain to be written on what the Council of Fifty meant to early Latter-day Saints and how the council's minutes shed new light on a myriad of topics in early Mormon and US history.

NOTES

1. Council of Fifty, Minutes, March 11 and April 18, 1844, in Matthew J. Grow, Ronald K. Esplin, Mark Ashurst-McGee, Gerrit J. Dirkmaat, and Jeffrey D. Mahas, eds., *Council of Fifty, Minutes, March 1844–January 1846*, vol. 1 of the Administrative Records series of *The Joseph Smith Papers*, ed. Ronald K. Esplin, Matthew J. Grow, and Matthew C. Godfrey (Salt Lake City: Church Historian's Press, 2016), 40, 128 (hereafter *JSP*, CFM).

2. See Klaus J. Hansen, *Quest for Empire: The Political Kingdom of God and the Council of Fifty in Mormon History* ([East Lansing]: Michigan State University Press, 1967); D. Michael Quinn, "The Council of Fifty and Its Members, 1844 to 1945," *BYU Studies* 20, no. 2 (Winter 1980): 163–97; Andrew F. Ehat, "'It Seems Like Heaven Began on Earth': Joseph Smith and the Constitution of the Kingdom of God," *BYU Studies* 20, no. 3 (Spring 1980): 253–80; and Jedediah S. Rogers, ed., *The Council of Fifty: A Documentary History* (Salt Lake City: Signature Books, 2014).

3. See Robin Scott Jensen, Robert J. Woodford, and Steven C. Harper, eds., *Manuscript Revelation Books*, facsimile edition, vol. 1 of the Revelations and Translations series of *The Joseph Smith Papers*, ed. Dean C. Jessee, Ronald K. Esplin, and Richard Lyman Bushman (Salt Lake City: Church Historian's Press, 2009).

4. R. Scott Lloyd, "Newest Volume Published for the Joseph Smith Papers Project," *Church News*, September 16, 2013.

5. See, for instance, Donald Q. Cannon, "Spokes on the Wheel: Early Latter-day Saint Settlements in Hancock County, Illinois," *Ensign*, February 1986, 62–68; Glen M. Leonard, "The Gathering to Nauvoo, 1839–45," *Ensign*, April 1979, 35–42; Reed Durham, "What Is the Hosanna Shout?" in "Q&A: Questions and Answers," *New Era*, September 1973, 14–15; and Ronald K. Esplin, "A 'Place Prepared' in the Rockies," *Ensign*, July 1988, 6–13.

6. The essays by Bushman, Reeve, and Bennett were first presented at the June 2016 MHA conference. The essays by Turley and Oman were first presented at the September 2016 University of Virginia conference. Several of these essays were then revised by their authors specifically for this compilation.

Chapter 1

THE SEPARATIST IMPULSE IN THE NAUVOO COUNCIL OF FIFTY

Richard Lyman Bushman

The publication of the Council of Fifty minutes as the first volume of the Administrative Records series in *The Joseph Smith Papers* can only be described as a triumph. The new volume is sure to be celebrated for its annotation and editing, another excellent addition to the papers project. But the minutes are also a triumph of the new transparency policy of the Church History Department. Over the years, the council minutes attained almost legendary status, as a trove of dark secrets sequestered in the recesses of the First Presidency's vault. Now the minutes have been published for all to examine.

When I was finishing up *Rough Stone Rolling*, my associate Jed Woodworth once asked if I could rest easy with my accounting of Joseph Smith's life without having examined the Council of Fifty minutes. At the time, I brushed aside his concern, feeling we knew enough about Nauvoo already. Now I am not so sure. The minutes do shed light on questions about the last days of Nauvoo that could not be answered before. None of the topics the council addressed are completely new. They all grew out of ongoing issues in the Church's history: protecting the Church from mobs, dealing with Indians, preparing for westward migration, establishing the kingdom of God in the last days. But the minutes reveal how desperate and angry the leaders were and how far they were willing to go.

My particular interest is to solve a puzzle inherent in the history as we have long understood it. Was the Church in Nauvoo committed to the

United States as a host government or not? In the spring of 1844, Joseph Smith ran for the office of president, implying that the government and the Constitution were worthy institutions under which the Saints were prepared to dwell. At the same time, the Saints were planning migrations to Texas, California, and Oregon, outside the boundaries of the United States, as if they were prepared to jump ship and build their kingdom out from under the nation's oversight. Their intentions were made clear when they scratched Texas from the list of possible destinations after it was absorbed into the Union. They wanted to leave the United States.

So which is it? Did the Mormons wish to strengthen their ties with the government, or were they ready to throw it over and strike out on their own?

The council's papers don't offer a definitive yes or no answer to these questions. In the spring of 1844, the council sent off a petition to the federal government for authorization to lead an army into the West. They proposed that Joseph Smith command one hundred thousand troops stationed along the migration routes to protect Americans moving west. It appears that the Saints were willing to collaborate with the federal government when it served their purposes. In their frame of mind, they seemed able to pursue two opposing courses of action at once. If they could plant crops and build the temple while laying plans to move west, then they could cooperate with the government while laying plans to separate.

But if ties were never severed completely, the strongest impression from the rhetoric William Clayton recorded in the minutes was of men ready to abandon the United States. The anger the Saints felt at the abuses they had suffered and at the impotence of government in rescuing them boils to the surface time and again. In places the language was excruciating. Perhaps much of their rhetoric was froth, not hard policy. But they gave vent repeatedly and passionately. Beneath their appeals for a refuge lay a deep anger. Brigham Young for one said he felt the day was past for preaching the gospel in the United States. "He dont care about preaching to the gentiles any longer," Clayton wrote of Young.[1] Their treatment of the Saints disqualified them. The council members were convinced that their persecutors would never be brought to justice. Amasa Lyman said that whenever "he thinks of the government he thinks 'damn it'. There has been nothing but one continued scene of wrath and persecution poured upon us. They legislate for pe[r]secution."[2]

The minute books of the Nauvoo Council of Fifty. The minutes were published in 2016 by *The Joseph Smith Papers*. Photograph by Welden C. Andersen. Courtesy of Church History Library, Salt Lake City.

Lyman certainly spoke for Brigham Young. "As to suffering any more of the oppression and tyranny of the gentiles," Young said, "just so soon as we can secure our women and children and put them where they will be safe, we will put our warriors into the field and never cease our operations untill we have swept the scoundrels off from the face of the earth."[3]

When the prospect of war with the United States could be anticipated with equanimity and even satisfaction, the proclivities of these men were evident. Prophecy told them an independent kingdom would be established before the Second Coming, and this was the moment. Wrote Clayton on March 11, 1844, "All seemed agreed to look to some place where we can go and establish a Theocracy either in Texas or Oregon or somewhere in California."[4] Small wonder they insisted on confidentiality. They knew they were speaking treason, much as Samuel Adams and the Boston patriots had in 1775. The council was prepared to declare the Mormons' independence from the United States. As Brigham Young put it in May 1845, "When we go from here we dont calculate to go under any government but the government of God."[5]

As time went by, practical necessity dictated collaboration with the government. Church leaders never quite went for complete independence. But if prudence required cooperation, we cannot believe that the passion of the Council of Fifty died away immediately. That separatist urge, that rage against injustice, that despair of ever finding security under the federal government must have lived on in many hearts. The 1857 invasion by an American army would only feed their fears and resentments. Restive spirits must have harbored a desire for a complete break—or at least as much independence as possible.

The question then becomes: How did these separatist impulses find expression in nineteenth-century Utah, and how were they finally put to rest? If progress was made as the decades went by, then federal intervention in the 1860s and 1870s and hostile action in the 1880s could only have revived the Saints' disaffection. It cannot be a coincidence that John Taylor, also a militant in 1845, reconstituted the Council of Fifty at the moment when the antipolygamy laws were to be enforced. We have long understood the suspicions of the Saints toward the federal government throughout the nineteenth century. The Council of Fifty minutes require us to recognize how strong those apprehensions were.

In the end, the Saints gave way to the government. Under the pragmatic Wilford Woodruff, polygamy was abandoned, and theocratic government was dissolved. Their hostile countrymen were not allowed to grind the Saints into the dust. The Saints merged into the American political system, including participation in the competing political parties. Joseph F. Smith insisted in the Smoot hearings that the Mormons were prepared to play by American rules. The Saints themselves acted the part of hyperpatriots, declaring their utter loyalty to the government and enlisting enthusiastically in the armed services during World War I.

But how long did it take for the anger of the fifty men gathered in council in Nauvoo in 1844 to dissipate? What part did these separatist impulses play in nineteenth-century Utah? It is hard today to imagine their rage and despair, but their words are on record and have been made public. We will now have to decide what they mean for Mormon history.

NOTES

1. Council of Fifty, Minutes, March 11, 1845, in Matthew J. Grow, Ronald K. Esplin, Mark Ashurst-McGee, Gerrit J. Dirkmaat, and Jeffrey D. Mahas, eds., *Council of Fifty, Minutes, March 1844–January 1846*, vol. 1 of the Administrative Records series of *The Joseph Smith Papers*, ed. Ronald K. Esplin, Matthew J. Grow, and Matthew C. Godfrey (Salt Lake City: Church Historian's Press, 2016), 299 (hereafter *JSP*, CFM).
2. Council of Fifty, Minutes, March 18, 1845, in *JSP*, CFM:336.
3. Council of Fifty, Minutes, March 18, 1845, in *JSP*, CFM:328.
4. Council of Fifty, Minutes, March 11, 1844, in *JSP*, CFM:40.
5. Council of Fifty, Minutes, March 1, 1845, in *JSP*, CFM:268.

Chapter 2

INJUSTICES LEADING TO THE CREATION OF THE COUNCIL OF FIFTY

Richard E. Turley Jr.

On the morning of September 25, 1824, Joseph Smith Sr. and some of his neighbors stood, shovels in hand, next to the grave where just ten months earlier, the Smith family had buried the remains of Alvin Smith. The agonizing death of Alvin at the age of twenty-five was still fresh in the minds of Joseph and Lucy Mack Smith and their children. Purposefully, the men at the grave thrust their shovels into the dark soil and began tossing earth to the side, digging deeper and deeper, hoping to hear their tools strike something hard, wooden, and hollow. When at last they found and uncovered the casket, they pried open the lid and peered in. There, much to their relief, they found Alvin's remains, partially decomposed but undisturbed.

Later that day, after reinterring his son's body, Joseph Sr. went to the office of the *Wayne Sentinel* newspaper and filed a report that was published two days later. Addressed "To the Public," it countered rumors that Alvin's remains had been removed and "dissected." Such rumors had been "peculiarly calculated to harrow up the mind of a parent and deeply wound the feelings of relations." As such, Joseph Sr. pleaded with those who circulated the rumor to stop.[1]

The original gravestone of Alvin Smith, brother of Joseph Smith, is encased on the back side of this newer marker. Photograph by Brent R. Nordgren.

What could have sparked such an incident? It began four years earlier, when Joseph Smith Jr. reported his First Vision to a trusted religious leader in his area. "I was greatly surprised at his behavior," Joseph reported. "He treated my communication not only lightly, but with great contempt, saying it was all of the devil." And it didn't end there. "I soon found . . . that my telling the story had excited a great deal of prejudice against me," Joseph wrote, "and was the cause of great persecution."[2]

In the years that followed, Joseph wrote, "rumor with her thousand tongues was all the time employed in circulating falsehoods about my father's family, and about myself. If I were to relate a thousandth part of them, it would fill up volumes."[3] It was one of these rumors that convinced Father Smith to confirm that Alvin's body had not been stolen.

Throughout Joseph Smith Jr.'s life, persecution followed his religious claims. His search for protection for himself and his followers led to two decisions in the final months of his life: to run for president of the United States and to form the Council of Fifty. In his candidacy for the presidency, he strongly advocated for religious liberty for all Americans, not just for Latter-day Saints. In the Council of Fifty, he discussed the creation of a theocracy outside the borders of the United States that would be defined by its extension of religious liberty to all individuals. This essay contextualizes those decisions in the opposition against the Latter-day Saints, with an emphasis on the 1830s. There were other immediate antecedents for the Council of Fifty and complex causes for its establishment in 1844. Nevertheless, the experiences of Mormons during the 1830s indelibly shaped their mindset on the necessity of religious liberty, the failure of current governments to adequately protect it, and the need for a new type of government to defend the liberty of Latter-day Saints and other religious minorities.

OPPOSITION IN JACKSON COUNTY

While early Mormons had already experienced intense opposition by 1833, their experience that year in Missouri exemplified how far their opponents were willing to go. By that time, thousands of Saints had flocked to Jackson County, Missouri, which one of Joseph Smith's revelations had designated as the place to build "Zion." They soon encountered opposition from those who disliked their religious views and also clashed culturally with them. For instance, most of the Saints who moved into Jackson County were northerners, meaning they did not favor slavery, unlike many of their Missouri neighbors.

As opposition to the Saints increased, some Missourians began to vandalize Mormon property and exhibit other signs of prejudice against members of this minority faith. Those with the greatest prejudice began looking for something they could use as a pretense for driving out the members of the Church.

Religious, cultural, economic, and political tensions exploded after the Church's newspaper in Missouri ran an article advising free blacks coming into the state how to avoid encountering trouble with Missouri's laws. The article provided the pretense that vigilantes needed to rally support for their cause against the Saints and wreak violence on them.

Resorting to patriotic language, vigilantes drafted a constitution or mob manifesto to draw sympathizers to their cause. As is so often the case with vigilantes, the Missouri mobbers cloaked their extralegal activities in patriotic language. Following the rhetoric of the Declaration of Independence, which concluded with the signers pledging "to each other our Lives, our Fortunes, and our sacred Honor," the mobbers concluded their manifesto with similar words: "We agree to use such means as may be sufficient to remove them [the Mormons], and to that end we each pledge to each other our bodily powers, our lives, fortunes and sacred honors."[4]

After demanding that the Mormons leave immediately and giving them only a short time to respond, the vigilantes attacked the most senior Church leader in the area, Bishop Edward Partridge, kidnapping him from his home, battering him repeatedly, partially stripping off his clothes, and daubing him in tar and feathers.

A group of vigilantes also attacked the Saints' printing establishment, a sturdy two-story brick structure. They evicted the printer's family and tore the building completely to the ground, stopping the publication of the first volume of Joseph Smith's revelations and of the newspaper *The Evening and the Morning Star*.

In the face of such violence, Church leaders agreed that their people would leave. Later, they reconsidered and decided to seek legal redress for the crimes committed against them and to defend their rights as US citizens.

Irked at the Saints' legal efforts, the vigilantes intensified the violence. One of the Church members, Lyman Wight, later testified:

> Some time towards the last of the summer of 1833, they commenced their operations of mobocracy. . . . [G]angs of from thirty to sixty, visit[ed] the house of George Bebee, calling him out of his house at the hour of midnight, with many guns and pistols pointed at his breast, beating him most inhuman[e]ly with clubs and whips; and the same night or night afterwards, this gang unroofed thirteen houses in what was called the Whitmer Branch of the Church in Jackson county. These scenes of mobocracy continued to exist with unabated fury. Mobs went from house to house, thrusting poles and rails in at the windows and doors of the houses of the Saints, tearing down a number of houses, turning hogs, horses, &c., into cornfields, burning fences, &c.[5]

In October, Wight recounted, the mobbers broke into a Mormon-owned store. When Wight, along with thirty or forty Mormons, went to the scene, he "found a man name of McArty [Richard McCarty], brickbatting the store door with all fury, the silks, calicoes, and other fine goods, entwined about his feet, reaching within the door of the store house." After McCarty was arrested, he was quickly acquitted. The next day, the Mormons who had testified against McCarty were arrested on charges of false imprisonment and "by the testimony of this one burglar, were found guilty, and committed to jail."[6]

Used to being treated like a full-fledged citizen before joining the Church, Wight now felt his civil rights were being violated. "This so exasperated my feelings," he said, "that I went with two hundred men to enquire into the affair, when I was promptly met by the colonel of the militia, who stated to me that the whole had been a religious farce, and had grown out of a prejudice they had imbibed against said Joseph Smith, a man with whom they were not acquainted."[7]

Hoping to de-escalate the violence, Wight agreed that the Saints would give up their arms if the militia colonel

> would take the arms from the mob. To this the colonel cheerfully agreed, and pledged his honor with that of Lieutenant Governor [Lilburn W.] Boggs . . . and others. This treaty entered into, we returned home, resting assured on their honor, that we would not be farther molested. But this solemn contract was violated in every sense of the word. The arms of the mob were never taken away, and the majority of the militia, to my certain knowledge, was engaged the next day with the mob, ([the colonel and] Boggs not excepted,) going from house to house in gangs of sixty to seventy in number, threatening the lives of [Mormon] women and children, if they did not leave forthwith.[8]

Church member Barnet Cole later signed an affidavit explaining what happened to him. According to his affidavit, three armed men accosted him at his house and compelled him to "go out a pace with them," telling him "some gentleman wished to see him." He was forced to a spot "where there were from forty to fifty men armed."

One of the armed men asked his kidnappers, "Is this mister Cole?"

"Yes," one replied.

Challenging Barnet's religious views, an armed man asked him, "Do you believe in the book of Mormon?"

"Yes," he replied.

Swearing, the leader said, "That is enough. Give it to him."

The mob stripped off some of his clothes, "laid on ten lashes" as a warning, and then told him he could go home. Barnet did not leave the area, and some five weeks later, a mob came "into his house and gave him a second Whiping and ordered him to leave the County or it would be worse for him." He then left for Clay County.[9]

With all the Jackson County violence in late 1833, men, women, and children were chased from their homes, and they scrambled for their lives. Lyman Wight testified: "I saw one hundred and ninety women and children driven thirty miles across the prairie, with three decrepit men only in their company, in the month of Nov., the ground thinly crusted with sleet, and I could easily follow their trail by the blood that flowed from their lacerated feet!! on the stubble of the burnt prairie." He also described how the mob burned down all the Mormon homes in Jackson County.[10]

Despite the continual threat of violence, some Mormons returned to Jackson County. Lyman and Abigail Leonard returned to avoid starving to death. Abigail recalled, "A company of men armed with whips and guns about fifty or sixty came to the house. . . . Five of the numbered entered. . . . They ordered my husband to leave the house threatning to shoot him if he did not, he not complying with their desires, one of the five took a chair, and struck him upon the head, knocking him down, and then dragging him out of the house. I in the mean time beging of them to spare his li[f]e."

Abigail tried to save her husband, but three of the men aimed guns at her and swore to shoot her if she resisted further. "While this was transpiring," she said, one of the men "jumped upon my husband with his heels, my husband then got up they striping his clothes all from him excepting his pantaloons, then five or six attacked him with whips and gun sticks, and whipped him until he could not stand but fell to the ground."[11] They "beat and whipt" him "until [his] life," she said, "was almost extinct."[12]

APPEALS FOR PROTECTION AND REDRESS

One of the challenges the Saints faced during this time period was that their appeals for protection from the government went unheeded, in part because the officials who should have protected them either participated in the mobbings themselves or were sympathetic to those who did. The Saints then sought redress in the courts, only to face similar frustrations.

For example, when Edward Partridge initiated legal proceedings against those who tarred and feathered him, the leaders of the mob could not deny what they had done, since there were so many witnesses to the highly public event. Instead, despite kidnapping, assaulting, and battering the bishop, with no legal provocation on his part, the attackers claimed that they did it in self-defense.

The defense was so ludicrous that even the judge, a mob sympathizer, could not in good conscience accept the attackers' self-defense claim. So he did the next best thing for the mobbers. He ruled in favor of Partridge but awarded him only a penny and a peppercorn.[13]

No wonder the Saints grew frustrated. They were following the rules that were supposed to protect citizens, but because of their status as members of a despised minority faith, the law did not protect them from violence or provide redress after it occurred.

TEMPORARY REFUGE IN CLAY COUNTY

The Saints who were driven out of Jackson County sought refuge in Clay County, which was north across the Missouri River. There they found a measure of sympathy among some of the citizens.[14] Meanwhile, Lyman Wight rode long distances trying to find others who would sympathize with his fellow Saints and come to their aid. He later testified:

> I left my family for the express purpose of making an appeal to the American people to know something of the toleration of such vile and inhuman conduct, and travelled one thousand and three hundred miles through the interior of the United States, and was frequently answered "That such conduct was not justifiable in a republican government; yet we feel to say that we fear that Joe Smith is a very bad man, and circumstances alter cases. We would not wish to prejudge a man, but in some circumstances, the voice of the people ought to rule."[15]

Such replies reflected a problem in the United States at the time. The ruling majority could often do more or less as it pleased, even if that meant violating the civil rights of minorities. The minorities were expected to bend before the collective prejudice of the majority and could do little to protect themselves or obtain justice in the courts.

The agitators in Jackson County began making so much noise against the Mormons in Clay County that it affected the Saints' sympathizers there, who wanted to avoid trouble for themselves and their communities.[16] In addition, the impoverished refugees from Jackson County had begun working for the Clay County citizens, and as the Saints began to prosper economically and were joined by fellow Saints from elsewhere, they began to have, by virtue of their numbers, political power as well. This incited jealousies. Lyman Wight recalled that "when the Saints commenced purchasing some small possessions for themselves; this together with the emigration created a jealousy on the part of the old citizens that we were to be their servants no longer." Wight went on to describe gruesome whippings and beatings that were visited on the Saints.[17]

Once again, those who inflicted this violence on the Saints justified their crimes under the guise of patriotism. One mobber, who seemed to consider himself an upstanding citizen, wrote to family members about the violence he helped inflict. "We are trampling on our law and Constitution," he admitted in his letter, "but we Cant Help it in no way while we possessed the Spirit of 76," he claimed. "Six of our party . . . went to a mormon town. Several mormons Cocked their guns & Swore they would Shoot them. After Some Scrimiging two white men took a mormon out of Company & give him 100 lashes & it is thought he will Die of this Beating."[18] The almost matter-of-fact way that the mobber includes this description in a family letter is chilling.

To avoid further trouble, the Saints left Clay County and settled in Caldwell County, a new county established by sympathetic Missouri state legislators as a "sort of Mormon reservation."[19] At first, this seemed to settle the violence, but not for long.

THE MORMON WAR AND THE EXTERMINATION ORDER

Latter-day Saint men who went to vote at Gallatin, Missouri, faced opposition and fought back, winning the election-day fight but giving their critics just what they wanted—a reason to label them dangerous and to call for driving them out once again. What followed has been called the 1838 "Mormon War," a series of skirmishes (some deadly) between Missouri vigilantes and militiamen on one side and Latter-day Saints on the other.

In De Witt, Carroll County, vigilantes demanded that the Mormons leave and organized a "safety committee," appealing to other counties for "aid to remove Mormons, abolitionists, and other disorderly persons."[20] A

Parley P. Pratt was one of several members of the Church who wrote import-
ant accounts of the persecutions experienced by Church members in Missouri.
Photograph, circa 1850–56, likely by Marsena Cannon or Lewis W. Chaffin.
Courtesy of History Library, Salt Lake City.

Missouri newspaper reported these actions and, though sympathetic to
the vigilantes, commented, "By what color of propriety a portion of the
people of the State, can organize themselves into a body, independent of
the civil power, and contravene the general laws of the land by preventing

the free enjoyment of the right of citizenship to another portion of the people, we are at a loss to comprehend."[21]

The De Witt Mormons appealed to Governor Lilburn W. Boggs and a Missouri militia general to save them from extermination. The general brought his men and ordered the mob to disperse. The vigilantes refused, however, and the general's men threatened to join the mob. The general had to withdraw his troops and wrote to his superior officer, asking the governor to intervene.

Governor Boggs, who had participated in the expulsion of the Saints from Jackson County and valued his political position, ignored his duty to protect the Saints, saying that the "quarrel was between the Mormons and the mob."[22] Abandoning all hope of government protection, some four hundred Saints of De Witt, who had suffered intense hunger during the siege, fled the area, leaving behind valuable property that fell into the hands of their persecutors. During their flight to safety, some died.[23]

Other Saints in northwestern Missouri also suffered. In 1838, Asahel Lathrop purchased a land claim and settled down, "supposing," as he said, "that I was at peace with all men." On August 6, however, he joined other Mormon men in defending their right to vote at Gallatin. Before long, other men threatened to kill him if he did not leave the area. Some of his family members were sick at the time and could not easily be moved. His wife pleaded for him to leave the children with her and flee for his life. He hesitated but finally gave in to her pleadings.

Not long after he left, a mob of fourteen or fifteen men occupied his home and, as he later testified, "abus[ed] my family in almost every form that Creturs in the shape of human Beeings could invent." One of his children soon died. After appealing to local authorities for protection, he returned home to find the other members of his family "in a soriful situation not one of the remaining ones able to wait uppon the other." He moved them sixty miles away, but his wife and two other family members soon died due to the "trouble and the want of care which they were deprived of by a Ruthless Mob."[24]

Left on their own, the Saints did their best to defend themselves and went on the offensive, making preemptive strikes to eliminate threats, disarm the enemy, and resupply their own people. A group of Missouri militia began driving Latter-day Saint families from their homes and took three prisoners. Several Mormons mobilized to rescue them before their rumored execution and ended up in a firefight that became known as the Battle of Crooked River. Although Mormon casualties exceeded those of the Missourians, exaggerated rumors reached Governor Boggs and led him to issue an order to exterminate or drive the Mormons from the state.[25]

A short time later, a large group of armed Missourians attacked the village of Hawn's Mill, which was occupied primarily by Latter-day Saints. Ignoring cries for mercy, the attackers killed seventeen men and boys and wounded many others. Before blowing off the head of a young boy found hiding under the bellows in the blacksmith shop, one vigilante uttered the slogan used for generations by bigots to justify the killing of the children of minorities: "Nits will make lice." The killers then plundered the village.[26]

FLIGHT TO ILLINOIS

With the upswell in violence, Saints in outlying areas fled to the Mormon capital of Far West for protection. There they waited, hoping that the government would intervene and rescue them. Instead, they were surrounded by troops, their leaders captured, and the people forced to sign over their property to pay the costs of the war. They were ordered to leave the state or face further violence. Over the course of the fall and winter, thousands of Saints braved harsh conditions to flee east across the prairie and over the Mississippi River. Meanwhile, Joseph Smith and his fellow prisoners listened to guards taunting them with stories of abuse heaped on Mormon victims.[27]

Writing from the Liberty jail, Joseph Smith and his fellow prisoners wrote of what they called "a lamentable tail[,] yea a sorrifull tail too much to tell[,] too much for contemplation[,] too much to think of for a moment[,] too much for human beings." Recounting some of the war's atrocities, they wrote of a Mormon man who was "mangled for sport" and of Latter-day Saint women who were robbed "of all that they have their last morsel for subsistance and then . . . violated to gratify the hellish desires of the mob and finally left to perish with their helpless of[f]spring clinging around their necks."[28]

Joseph, his brother Hyrum, and their companions later escaped to Illinois, where they joined many of the other refugee Saints, though Joseph never felt entirely safe there, as Missouri officials tried time and again to recapture and bring him back to what likely would have been execution.

The Saints tried to obtain justice for those who were killed and wounded, as well as compensation for the thousands whose property was taken from them. But all to no avail. Joseph even went to Washington, where he spoke with President Martin Van Buren. The president was sympathetic but thought the federal government had no power in the matter. Besides, he said, if he were to help the Mormons, he would lose the vote of the state of Missouri. In effect, he said, "Your cause is just, but I can do nothing for you."[29]

Based on these experiences, the Saints figured that if they were to have fairness and justice, they needed to have their own government, their own courts, and their own state-sanctioned militia. In the new settlement they established in Illinois, named Nauvoo, Mormons were the majority, and Joseph Smith became leader of the city, the court, and the militia. The city grew and prospered, aided by an influx of immigrant converts, and Joseph continued to seek equality and justice for his people. In late 1843, Joseph wrote the leading US presidential candidates, inquiring what they would do to protect the rights of Latter-day Saints. After getting unsatisfactory answers, he decided in early 1844 to run for president, with Sidney Rigdon as vice presidential candidate. Joseph's presidential campaign would be a way to draw attention to the plight of Saints, slaves, prisoners, debtors, and other downtrodden peoples. These events, as well as others in the early Nauvoo years, also provided crucial context for the establishment of the Council of Fifty in March 1844. A few months later, a mob killed Joseph and his brother Hyrum.

A FEW CLOSING OBSERVATIONS

First, although Latter-day Saints sometimes fought back and at times even went on the offensive, they were overwhelmingly the victims of illegal and extralegal violence. Second, the three branches of government failed to protect the Saints before they became victims or to compensate them for their losses afterward. Third, as is so often the case with groups who have minority status, the Mormons were victims of structural bias. In general, when they did wrong, they were punished harshly. But when others wronged them, even severely, they were not punished at all.

This history of repeated injustices suffered by the Latter-day Saints provides essential background to understanding the establishment of the Council of Fifty—a body that was designed, as Joseph Smith put it, "to be got up for the safety and salvation of the saints by protecting them in their religious rights and worship."[30]

NOTES

1. "To the Public," *Wayne Sentinel* (Palmyra, NY), October 27, 1824.
2. Joseph Smith—History 1:21–23, 27.
3. Joseph Smith—History 1:61.
4. "To His Excellency, Daniel Dunklin, Governor of the State of Missouri," *Evening and Morning Star* 2, no. 15 (December 1833): 228.
5. Lyman Wight, Testimony, *Times and Seasons* 4, no. 17 (1843): 262.
6. Wight, Testimony, 262.
7. Wight, Testimony, 262.
8. Wight, Testimony, 262.
9. Barnet Cole, Affidavit of January 7, 1840, in *Mormon Redress Petitions: Documents of the 1833–1838 Missouri Conflict*, vol. 16 of the Religious Studies Center Monograph Series, ed. Clark V. Johnson (Provo, UT: Religious Studies Center, 1992): 431–32.
10. Wight, Testimony, 263.
11. Abigail Leonard, Affidavit of March 11, 1840, in *Mormon Redress Petitions*, 273–74.
12. See unsworn, undated petition of Lyman Leonard in *Mormon Redress Petitions*, 699.
13. Karen Lynn Davidson, Richard L. Jensen, and David J. Whittaker, eds., *Histories, Volume 2: Assigned Histories, 1831–1847*, vol. 2 of the Histories series of *The Joseph Smith Papers*, ed. Dean C. Jessee, Ronald K. Esplin, and Richard Lyman Bushman (Salt Lake City: Church Historian's Press, 2012), 209, 227 (hereafter *JSP*, H2).

14. Parley P. Pratt et al., "'The Mormons' So Called," *The Evening and the Morning Star*, Extra, February 1834, [2].

15. Wight, Testimony, 263.

16. Edward Partridge, "A History, of the Persecution, of the Church of Jesus Christ, of Latter Day Saints in Missouri," *Times and Seasons* 1, no. 4 (1840): 50, in *JSP*, H2:226.

17. Wight, Testimony, 263.

18. Durward T. Stokes, ed., "The Wilson Letters, 1835–1849," *Missouri Historical Review* 60, no. 4 (July 1966): 508–9. On the writer's distinction between "white men" and "a mormon," see W. Paul Reeve, *Religion of a Different Color: Race and the Mormon Struggle for Whiteness* (New York: Oxford University Press, 2015).

19. *Chicago Times*, August 7, 1875, https://en.wikisource.org/wiki/Chicago_Times, _August_7, 1875.

20. "Anti-Mormons," *Missouri Republican* (St. Louis), August 1838, in *Publications of the Nebraska State Historical Society: Volume XX*, ed. Albert Watkins (Lincoln: Nebraska State Historical Society, 1922), 80.

21. "The Mormons," *Southern Advocate* (Jackson, MO), September 1, 1838, https://web.archive.org/web/20110515042529/http://www.sidneyrigdon.com/dbroad hu/MO/Miss1838.htm.

22. "Extract, from the Private Journal of Joseph Smith Jr.," in *Times and Seasons* 1, no. 1 (1839): 2–9, josephsmithpapers.org/paper-summary/extract-from-the -private-journal-of-joseph-smith-jr-july-1839/1.

23. "Trial of Joseph Smith," *Times and Seasons* 4, no. 17 (1843): 257; Joseph Smith, History, 1838–1856, vol. B-1, 836, josephsmithpapers.org/paper-summary/hist ory-1838-1856-volume-b-1-1-september-1834-2-november-1838/290.

24. Asahel A. Lathrop, Affidavit of May 8, 1839, and March 17, 1840, in *Mormon Redress Petitions,* 263–66.

25. Lilburn W. Boggs to John B. Clark, October 27, 1838, Mormon War Papers, Missouri State Archives, Jefferson City.

26. *History of Caldwell and Livingston Counties, Missouri: Written and Compiled from the Most Authentic Official and Private Sources, including a History of Their Townships, Towns and Villages* (St. Louis: National Historical, 1886), 149.

27. "Memorial to the Missouri Legislature," January 24, 1839, Joseph Smith Letterbook 2, 66–67, josephsmithpapers.org/paper-summary/memorial-to-the-missouri -legislature-24-january-1839/1.

28. Joseph Smith to the Church and Edward Partridge, March 20, 1839, 3, josephsmithpapers.org/paper-summary/letter-to-the-church-and-edward-part ridge-20-march-1839/3. See also the testimonies of Hyrum Smith, "Missouri vs Joseph Smith," *Times and Seasons* 4, no. 16 (1843): 255; and Parley P. Pratt, "Trial of Joseph Smith," *Times and Seasons* 4, no. 17 (1843): 258.

29. Joseph Smith to Hyrum Smith and High Council, December 5, 1839, Joseph Smith Letterbook 2, 85, josephsmithpapers.org/paper-summary/letter-to-hyrum-smith -and-nauvoo-illinois-high-council-5-december-1839/1.

30. Council of Fifty, Minutes, April 18, 1844, in Matthew J. Grow, Ronald K. Esplin, Mark Ashurst-McGee, Gerrit J. Dirkmaat, and Jeffrey D. Mahas, eds., *Council of Fifty, Minutes, March 1844–January 1846*, vol. 1 of the Administrative Records series of *The Joseph Smith Papers*, ed. Ronald K. Esplin, Matthew J. Grow, and Matthew C. Godfrey (Salt Lake City: Church Historian's Press, 2016), 128.

Chapter 3

THE COUNCIL OF FIFTY AND JOSEPH SMITH'S PRESIDENTIAL AMBITIONS

Spencer W. McBride

Discussion of Joseph Smith's 1844 presidential campaign elicits a fairly standard set of questions. Was Joseph Smith serious about his presidential ambitions or was he merely a protest candidate running to raise awareness of the Mormons' plight? Did Smith and his fellow Church leaders believe that he could actually win the election? If they did, how confident were they that the campaign strategy they had devised would carry Smith into the White House? For decades, scholars defended their respective answers to these questions with relatively limited source materials, reliant instead on their own interpretations of the few surviving statements that Smith and his close associates made concerning the seriousness of his campaign.[1] But the minutes of the Council of Fifty provide scholars with new source material on the presidential campaign that, when considered with sources previously known, better equips them to examine these key questions.

The Council of Fifty minutes reveal that Smith was more than a protest candidate—that is, that he and other Church leaders viewed an electoral triumph as possible, even if unlikely. While council members were certain that the campaigning efforts of Church leaders throughout the United States were essential to Smith's success, they appear to have believed that his candidacy would ultimately require some form of divine intervention in order to succeed. Yet the most significant aspect of Smith's presidential campaign illuminated by the Council of Fifty minutes is that the campaign was merely one possible avenue by which Latter-day Saints could attempt to obtain federal redress and protection while awaiting the establishment of the political kingdom of God. Smith's run for the American presidency thus represents a nexus of idealism and pragmatism as well as an unusual combination of providentialism and contingency planning.

REASONS FOR SMITH'S CAMPAIGN

Smith launched his presidential campaign on January 29, 1844, when he accepted the nomination made by Willard Richards, a member of the Quorum of the Twelve Apostles, in a meeting of Church leaders.[2] A few days later, after a public reading of his campaign pamphlet, *General Smith's Views on the Powers and Policy of the Government of the United States*, Smith justified his candidacy to his followers. "I would not have suffered my name to have been used by my friends on any wise as president of the United States or Candidate for that office," he explained, "if I and my friends could have had the privilege of enjoying our religious and civil rights as American citizens." But since he felt that his followers had been denied those rights, he declared, "I feel it to be my right and privilege to obtain what influence and power I can lawfully in the United States for the protection of injured innocence." In this same meeting, Smith called on "every man in the city who could speak" to go "throughout the land to electioneer," insisting that "there is oratory enough in the church to carry me into the presidential chair the first slide."[3]

While these words elucidate the reasons Smith was seeking the presidency, they do not clearly establish whether he was serious about the race or if he thought he could win. Indeed, various men and women have campaigned for the presidency without any expectation—or desire—to win but rather to raise awareness for the issues that mattered most to them and their followers.[4] In Smith's case, his presidential ambitions could bring the plight of the Mormons—first in Missouri and then in Illinois—to the attention of the American public as well as to savvy politicians who recognized the potential electoral boost they might receive as a result of supporting the Mormon's petitioning efforts with state and federal governments.

John Tyler was president of the United States at the time that Joseph Smith announced his own presidential campaign. Lithograph by Charles Fenderich. Courtesy of Library of Congress, Washington, DC.

THE COUNCIL OF FIFTY'S ROLE IN JOSEPH SMITH'S CAMPAIGN

The Council of Fifty assumed much of the responsibility for managing Smith's campaign. Committee members helped build the campaign message around the themes set forth in *General Smith's Views,* titling their independent presidential ticket "Jeffersonianism, Jeffersonian Democracy, free trade and Sailors rights, protection of person & property."[5] They also selected and invited men to be the vice presidential candidate on Smith's independent ticket. Their first choice was James Arlington Bennet of New York, who had corresponded with

Jeffersonian Democracy.

Protection of Person and Property.

For President,
JOSEPH SMITH.

For Vice President,
SIDNEY RIGDON.

Electors for the State of Michigan,
Mephibosheth Sirrine,
William Van Every,
Samuel Graham,
Alvan Hood,
Seth Taft.

Men campaigning for Joseph Smith issued tickets like this for use as ballots in the presidential election. Courtesy of Church History Library, Salt Lake City.

Smith for years and joined the church in 1843. However, after council members discovered—incorrectly—that Bennet was born in Ireland (and therefore ineligible for the vice presidency), they opted to invite Solomon Copeland, a friend to Church members in Tennessee, to assume that place on the ticket. When Copeland failed to respond to the council's invitation, council members decided to name Sidney Rigdon, a counselor in the Church's First Presidency, as Smith's running mate.[6]

MORE THAN A PROTEST CANDIDATE

The view of Smith as a mere protest candidate arose in the weeks immediately following his nomination, even among some of the Mormon leader's close friends and supporters. For instance, in responding to the invitation to run for vice president on Smith's ticket, Bennet wrote to Willard Richards that "if you can by any Supernatural means Elect Brother Joseph President of these [United] States, I have not a doubt that he would govern the people and administer the laws in good faith, and with righteous intentions, but I can see no Natural means by which he has the slightest chance of receiving the votes of even a one state." Considering other possible reasons for the campaign, Bennet continued: "If the object of [Smith's] friends be to aid the Cause of Mormonism in foreign lands, or in this Country among a certain class of persons . . . then I think they are somewhat in the right track, but if they are aiming in reality at that high office then I must say that at present they, in my opinion, are on a wild goose chase."[7]

Richards responded to Bennet in June. "Your views about the nomination of Gen. Smith for the presidency are correct," he wrote. "We will gain popularity and extend influence, but this is not all, we mean to elect him, and nothing shall be wanting on our part to accomplish it."[8] Richards clearly acknowledged the potential benefits of the presidential campaign toward raising awareness of the Mormons' plight but insisted that those benefits did not exclude an expectation of electoral success. Furthermore, his insistence that "there would be nothing wanting on our part to accomplish it" suggests that Smith's election would require help from an outside—even a divine—source.

Still, protest candidates do not always publicly identify themselves as such. That Smith and his fellow Mormon leaders were serious in putting his name forth as a presidential candidate is demonstrated by their efforts to select electors in a formal convention. At a meeting of the Council of Fifty on April 25, 1844, the council decided to "have delegates in all the electoral districts and hold a national convention at Baltimore," where both the Whig and Democratic Parties were holding their respective nominating conventions that May. Smith stated that "the easiest and the best way to accomplish the object in view is to make an effort to secure the election at this contest."[9] Indeed, at a conference of the Church just two weeks earlier, Church leaders had called for members "to preach the Gospel and Electioneer" for Smith. Nearly three hundred men volunteered, and volunteers were subsequently assigned to preach and campaign in specific states in which they would "appoint conferences . . . to get up electors who will go for [Smith] for the presidency."[10]

If the Church was promoting Smith's candidacy simply to raise public awareness for the plight of its members, then electors were superfluous. While it was common in the earliest American presidential elections for the legislatures of many states—and not the people—to select the men who eventually cast their votes in the Electoral College, by the 1840s only South Carolina still used this method to select its electors. The rest of the states had moved to a system in which the winner of the state's popular vote received the support of all of the electors allotted to it.[11] This meant that the selection of electors was a technical aspect in a strategy to *actually* elect someone president, an aspect that had little significance in a campaign focused solely on building public support for a cause. By designating a slate of electors in each state, Church leaders created an electoral infrastructure designed to convert popular support into the votes that could actually carry a person to the presidency. Of course, without popular support, that infrastructure would be useless.

The Council of Fifty's emphasis on securing electors in each state should Smith win the popular vote in those places illuminates the way the council viewed the presidential campaign. To council members, Smith was not merely a protest candidate. They thought that he could win and made the necessary technical arrangements to facilitate such an event should large numbers of Americans in each state cast their votes for him. After all, no amount of popular votes or divine intervention could make Smith president without the requisite number of electoral votes.

ALTERNATIVE SOLUTIONS

That Mormon leaders believed Smith *could* win the presidency did not necessarily mean that they believed he *would* win. It was merely one possible avenue through which they believed divine providence could work to restore the United States to its privileged place in God's grand plan for the world and to help the Saints reclaim their promised land of Zion. Despite Richards's insistence to James Arlington Bennet that the reason Church leaders were promoting Smith's candidacy for president was "because we are satisfied . . . that this is the best or only method of saving our free institutions from total overthrow," the Council of Fifty members were exploring several possible avenues that might eventually lead them to the peace and prosperity in the land they believed that God had promised to them while still remaining citizens of a country that had hitherto condoned their ill treatment.[12] For instance, the Council of Fifty petitioned the federal government to authorize Smith to form and lead a military force of one hundred thousand men to protect Texas and Oregon from foreign invasion. If Congress had agreed to the plan, Smith would presumably have become a general in the US Army—certainly a promotion from his role as lieutenant general of the Nauvoo Legion. The United States would have a force dedicated to protecting its interests in Texas and Oregon, and Smith would have an army at his command to ward off mobs that threatened the Mormons in Nauvoo.[13]

In addition, the council dispatched Heber C. Kimball and Lyman Wight to Washington, DC, in May 1844 to petition Congress for "a liberal grant of lands in one of the Territories of the United States, to be located in such manner as not to deprive any previous settler of any just right or claim." They asked that the government either give them the land outright or sell it to them on favorable terms of credit. Such an arrangement would have provided the Mormons a degree of isolation ideal for preventing future outbreaks of violence with non-Mormon neighbors, like those that occurred in Missouri during the 1830s or that appeared imminent in western Illinois in 1844.[14]

Yet another proposed solution was that the federal government designate Nauvoo a territory. In such a scenario, the city would effectively secede from Illinois and fall under the protection and direct authority of the federal government. Smith explained in an April meeting of the Council of Fifty that such an arrangement would "set us everlastingly free, and give us the United States troops to guard us and protect us from any invasion."[15] However far-fetched and unlikely the proposal may have been, territorial status would have empowered Smith and his followers to exercise greater sovereignty in governing their society in nonecclesiastical matters, the kind of sovereignty that was at that time eliciting suspicion and opposition from several prominent figures in Illinois politics.

Smith's election or any of these other plans would have provided substantial relief to the Mormons amid the growing hostility they felt from

The White House, circa 1846. Daguerreotype by John Plumbe. Courtesy of Library of Congress, Washington, DC.

their fellow citizens in Illinois. Yet the Council of Fifty members anticipated that all their plans to remain in the United States on their own terms
might fail. Accordingly, they planned for an exodus to a place where they
could establish themselves as a sovereign people.[16] In the end, Smith was
murdered several months before Election Day, and Congress never seriously considered any of the Mormon leadership's proposed plans. Moving
out of the country thus appeared to many council members as the plan
God intended for them to pursue.

CONCLUSION

Joseph Smith was not merely a protest candidate campaigning for the sole
purpose of raising awareness of the poor treatment of the Mormons in
a country that claimed to value religious liberty. While parties operating
outside the mainstream Whig and Democratic Parties often held conventions to *nominate* candidates, holding conventions designed to select electors in each state was less common. Still, as the intent of the Council of
Fifty was to "leave nothing wanting" on its part where the election was concerned, council members simultaneously planned for other contingencies,
working out an array of potential paths to the building up of the kingdom
of God on earth, a kingdom that they believed they were destined to lead.

NOTES

1.   Several scholars have examined Smith's campaign and offered their respective
     opinions on how serious Smith was about his presidential ambitions. Fawn
     Brodie wrote that Smith "suffered from no illusions about his chances of
     winning the supreme political post in the nation. He entered the ring not only
     to win publicity for himself and his church, but most of all to shock the other
     candidates into some measure of respect." Fawn Brodie, *No Man Knows My
     History: The Life of Joseph Smith*, 2nd ed. (New York: Knopf, 1971), 362. Richard
     Bushman portrays Smith's campaign largely as a gesture designed to attract pub-
     licity to the Church and its petitioning efforts but acknowledges that "with a
     large field of candidates and no clear favorite," Smith "may have thought he
     could gain votes through convert baptisms and steal the victory in a split vote."
     Richard Lyman Bushman, *Joseph Smith: Rough Stone Rolling* (New York: Knopf,

2005), 515. In setting forth their conspiracy theory that Smith was assassinated in order to elect Henry Clay president, Robert S. Wicks and Fred R. Foister portray Smith as a serious candidate with a real chance to win. Robert S. Wicks and Fred R. Foister, *Junius and Joseph: Presidential Politics and the Assassination of the First Mormon Prophet* (Logan: Utah State University Press, 2005). John Bicknell asserts that Smith "understood fully that he would not be elected president" but that "the campaign afforded him a chance to spread the word about Mormonism and put its case before the people and their leaders." John Bicknell, *America 1844: Religious Fervor, Westward Expansion, and the Presidential Election That Transformed the Nation* (Chicago: Chicago Review Press, 2015), 48–49; see also Newell G. Bringhurst, "Reflections on a Roundtable Colloquium Dealing with Joseph Smith's 1844 Campaign for U.S. President," *John Whitmer Historical Society Journal* 22 (2002): 153–58.

2. Joseph Smith, Journal, January 29, 1844, in Andrew H. Hedges, Alex D. Smith, and Brent M. Rogers, eds., *Journals, Volume 3: May 1843–June 1844*, vol. 3 of the Journals series of *The Joseph Smith Papers*, ed. Ronald K. Esplin and Matthew J. Grow (Salt Lake City: Church Historian's Press, 2015), 170.

3. Wilford Woodruff, Journal, February 8, 1844, in Scott G. Kenney, ed., *Wilford Woodruff's Journal: 1833–1898 Typescript* (Salt Lake City: Signature Books, 1983), 2:349.

4. Notable examples of American protest candidates include James G. Birney, the abolitionist and Liberty Party candidate in the presidential elections of 1840 and 1844, and Eugene V. Debs, the labor advocate and Socialist Party candidate in five of the six presidential elections between 1900 and 1920. On Birney and the Liberty Party, see Eric Foner, *Free Soil, Free Labor, and Free Men: The Ideology of the Republican Party before the Civil War* (New York: Oxford University Press, 1970), 78–82; and Vernon L. Volpe, "The Liberty Party and Polk's Election," *The Historian* 53, no. 4 (Summer 1991): 691–710. On Debs and the Socialist Party, see Nick Salvatore, *Eugene V. Debs: Citizen and Socialist* (Urbana: University of Illinois Press, 1982).

5. Council of Fifty, Minutes, April 11, 1844, in Matthew J. Grow, Ronald K. Esplin, Mark Ashurst-McGee, Gerrit J. Dirkmaat, and Jeffrey D. Mahas, eds., *Council of Fifty, Minutes, March 1844–January 1846*, vol. 1 of the Administrative Records series of *The Joseph Smith Papers*, ed. Ronald K. Esplin, Matthew J. Grow, and Matthew C. Godfrey (Salt Lake City: Church Historian's Press, 2016), 90 (hereafter *JSP*, CFM).

6. Council of Fifty, Minutes, March 21 and May 6, 1844, in *JSP*, CFM:57, 157–59.

7. James Arlington Bennet to Willard Richards, April 14, 1844, Willard Richards Journals and Papers, 1821–1854, Church History Library, Salt Lake City (hereafter CHL).

8. Willard Richards to James Arlington Bennet, June 20, 1844, Willard Richards Journals and Papers, 1821–1854, CHL.

9. Council of Fifty, Minutes, April 25, 1844, in *JSP*, CFM:133–34. Ultimately, a convention in Nauvoo on May 17, 1844, resolved to hold the proposed "National Convention at Baltimore" on July 13. However, Smith's murder on June 27 stripped the event of its core purpose. See *JSP*, CFM:133n404.

10. Historian's Office, General Church Minutes, April 9, 1844, CHL; Conference Assignments, *Nauvoo Neighbor*, April 17, 1844, [2]; *JSP*, CFM:134n406.

11. Robert G. Dixon Jr., "Electoral College Procedure," *The Western Political Quarterly* 3, no. 2 (June 1950), 215.

12. Willard Richards to James Arlington Bennet, June 20, 1844, Willard Richards Journals and Papers, 1821–1854, CHL.

13. Council of Fifty, Minutes, March 26, 1844, in *JSP*, CFM:66–72. Empowering the federal government to send troops into individual states to protect religious minorities from mob violence without the formal request of a state's governor was a prominent plank in Smith's campaign platform. See Joseph Smith, *General Smith's Views on the Powers and Policy of the Government of the United States* (Nauvoo, IL: John Taylor, 1844), 10.

14. Lyman Wight and Heber C. Kimball, Petition to US Senate and House of Representatives, 1844, Record Group 46, Records of the US Senate, National Archives, Washington, DC; *JSP*, CFM:162n516.

15. Nauvoo City Council, Minutes, December 8 and 21, 1843, and February 12, 1844, CHL; Hyrum Smith et al., Memorial to the US Senate and House of Representatives, December 21, 1843, Record Group 46, Records of the US Senate, National Archives, Washington, DC; Council of Fifty, Minutes, April 18, 1844, in *JSP*, CFM:127–28.

16. For more on the discussion in the Council of Fifty about relocating the main body of the Church to Oregon, see Council of Fifty, Minutes, March 1, 1845, in *JSP*, CFM:267—68; and Letters from Orson Hyde, April 25 and 26, 1844, in *JSP*, CFM:181–84. On the discussion in the council about relocating the main body of the Church to Texas, see Council of Fifty, Minutes, April 18, 1844, in *JSP*, CFM:115–16, 127–28.

Chapter 4

GOD AND THE PEOPLE RECONSIDERED

Further Reflections on Theodemocracy in Early Mormonism

Patrick Q. Mason

Joseph Smith's quixotic 1844 presidential campaign, which ended prematurely and tragically with his murder in June of that year, introduced into the Mormon and American lexicon the concept of "theodemocracy." In a ghostwritten article in the Latter-day Saint newspaper *Times and Seasons* outlining his political principles, Smith declared, "As the 'world is governed too much' and as there is not a nation of dynasty, now occupying the earth, which acknowledges Almighty God as their law giver, and as 'crowns won by blood, by blood must be maintained,' I go emphatically, virtuously, and humanely, for a THEODEMOCRACY, where God and the people hold the power to conduct the affairs of men in righteousness." Smith went on to say that such a "theodemocratic" arrangement would guarantee liberty, free trade, the protection of life and property, and indeed "unadulterated freedom" for all.[1]

I can't recall when I first encountered Smith's notion of theodemocracy, but I became particularly interested in the subject when, as a master's student in international peace studies at the University of Notre Dame, I took a course on democratic theory. A search of electronic databases containing early American imprints, newspapers, and other primary sources suggested that the word "theodemocracy" was not in wide circulation at the time, and perhaps that the concept was original to Smith (or his ghost-writer William W. Phelps). I wondered if theodemocracy might even constitute a uniquely Mormon contribution to political theory. What began as a course paper eventually culminated in my article "God and the People: Theodemocracy in Nineteenth-Century Mormonism," published in 2011 in the *Journal of Church and State*.[2] My research suggests that outside of Mormon circles the term has rarely if ever been invoked, with the prominent exception of the influential twentieth-century Pakistani Islamist author and political organizer Sayyid Abul A'la Maududi.[3]

"God and the People" was not intended to provide a comprehensive history of Mormon political thought—an ambitious project that has yet to be undertaken.[4] Nevertheless, within its rather narrowly tailored perspective, the article did attempt to contribute to important conversations in Mormon history, American political history, and democratic theory. I argued that the Mormon concept of theodemocracy was designed to mediate in a contemporaneous debate over how to best protect minority rights and religious liberty—subjects that were far from academic for the earliest generations of Latter-day Saints. That Mormons would even consider a notion such as theodemocracy suggests their complicated relationship with American political ideals, even at a time when those ideals were themselves complex and in flux. Latter-day Saints joined other Americans in reflecting on the meaning of freedom and how to guarantee its blessings for all, not only the majority. From their own experience and reading of the US Constitution, Mormons identified religious freedom as the first and most important freedom, and they sought a political theory and system that would prevent the abuses they had recently suffered in Missouri.

The irony is that the Latter-day Saints' proposed remedy was viewed by their opponents as equally if not more dangerous than the sociopolitical ills it sought to cure. As I wrote, "Each side accused the other of undermining democracy and basic liberties: Smith and the Mormons embraced a more robust application of revealed religion in the public sphere as the answer to the secular government's hostility to religious minorities' rights (namely their own), while anti-Mormon critics denounced the prophet as a tyrant and his politics as theocratic despotism."[5] Theodemocracy, then, provides an excellent window onto the antiliberal tradition in American politics.

The illiberalism of vigilantism and state-sponsored violence against a particular religious minority group was countered by the illiberalism of theodemocracy. A consideration of Mormon theodemocracy therefore fixes our gaze upon the contending illiberalisms of nineteenth-century American political thought and behavior.

I concluded my article by expressing skepticism about theodemocracy as a tenable political theory, arguing that *theos* would always trump *demos*, and that such a system would perpetually struggle with an inability to tolerate real dissent. The particular turns of Mormon history following Joseph Smith's death, and especially after Wilford Woodruff's 1890 Manifesto, meant that what began as a radical political idea informed by millenarian theology became domesticated and limited to applications within ecclesiastical government. In the twentieth century, theodemocracy became far less political, far more churchly, and thus far less dangerous.

THE ALIENATION OF CHURCH LEADERS

The recent publication of the Council of Fifty's minutes from the final months of Joseph Smith's life provides an opportunity to reappraise the arguments I made in my 2011 article.[6] A thorough review of the Joseph Smith–era minutes does not upend any of my claims, but they do provide further texture and depth to our understanding of early Mormon politics, history, and theology. In particular, the minutes reveal a core of Latter-day Saint leaders even more alienated from American society than I suggested in my article. It still holds true, as I argued, that "the ranks of Mormonism in its first decade were hardly filled with fanatic dissidents, revolutionaries, or theocrats."[7] But the Council of Fifty minutes make clear that by 1844, many of the leading men of Mormonism had adopted a more jaded view. John Taylor dimly reviewed "the positions and prospects of the different nations of the earth" (though his mental geography seemed limited to the United States and northern Europe) and later asserted that "this nation is as far fallen and degenerate as any nation under heaven."[8] William W. Phelps begrudgingly admitted there were "a few pearls" in the Declaration of Independence and US Constitution—which an 1833 revelation said was "established . . . by the hands of wise men whom I [God] have raised up unto this very purpose"—but also "a tremendous

William W. Phelps and other council members expressed bitter feelings toward the US government. Photograph, circa 1850–60, likely by Marsena Cannon. Courtesy of Church History Library, Salt Lake City.

sight of chaff." Whatever original inspiration there may have been in the nation's founding, Phelps said, "the boasted freedom of these U. States is gone, gone to hell."[9] Sidney Rigdon embraced the world's degenerate political condition as a harbinger of the apocalypse. "The nations of the earth are very fast approximating to an utter ruin and overthrow," he proclaimed. "All the efforts the nations are making will only tend to hasten on the final doom of the world and bring it to its final issue."[10] In recent years many scholars have emphasized the optimistic, progressive nature of early Mormon theology. Without discounting that positive strain of thought within the movement, the Council of Fifty minutes remind us that many early Mormons shared a rather dark view of the world that lay beyond gathered Zion, a pessimism founded upon Smith's millenarian revelations and fueled by the Missouri persecutions.[11]

The council members' alienation with present governments led to their openness to, and even enthusiasm for, a theocratic alternative. By focusing so intently on theodemocracy, my article underplayed the commitments of many early Mormon leaders to plain old theocracy. In the Council of Fifty's first meeting on March 11, 1844, clerk William Clayton recorded that "all seemed agreed to look to some place where we can go and establish a Theocracy."[12] Indeed, theocracy was built into the council's DNA from the beginning. Sidney Rigdon, Brigham Young, and other council members stood ready to ditch *demos* in favor of *theos* and the political rule of God's appointed servant, Joseph Smith. Rigdon asserted that the council's "design was to form a Theocracy according to the will of Heaven."[13] Brigham Young declared, "No line can be drawn between the church and other governments, of the spritual and temporal affairs of the church. Revelations must govern. The voice of God, shall be the voice of the people."[14] Later, Young argued that the government of the kingdom of God was in no need of a constitution so long as its subjects had Smith as their "Prophet, Priest and King," who represented "a perfect committee of himself" through whom God would speak.[15] One can see here the foundations of an authoritarian streak that has manifest itself throughout the larger Mormon tradition, whether it be in what historians have characterized as Young's "kingdom in the West" or the "one-man rule" that Rulon Jeffs introduced in the Fundamentalist Church of Jesus Christ of Latter-day Saints in the 1980s.[16]

Not all council members were so enthusiastic about theocracy. Almon Babbitt departed from his fellow council members to explain (and presumably defend) "laws in general" and especially "the laws of the land." He went so far as to remind his colleagues of "the apostacy of the children of Israel in choosing a king."[17] Babbitt's reservations notwithstanding, one can sense in the minutes an emergent groupthink as council members built upon one another's exuberance for the establishment of the political kingdom of God, confirming and even outperforming one another's earnest declarations.

At the same time, the minutes affirm that for all their theocratic illiberality, the council members were unanimously committed, at least in their own minds, to equal rights for all. They believed that "having sought in vain among all the nations of the earth, to find a government instituted by heaven; an assylum for the opprest; a protector of the innocent, and a shield for the defenceless," it was their God-given duty to create a government that would not only fulfill prophecy but also protect society's most vulnerable members.[18] At times their commentary was concerned primarily with self-protection and the maintenance of their own rights, but this special pleading did frequently give way to more universalistic sentiments. Religious freedom provided the foundation for their broader thinking about individual liberties and the limits of government power. For instance, Amasa Lyman opined that one of their chief purposes in establishing the government of the kingdom of God was to "secure the right of liberty in matters of conscience to men of every character, creed and condition in life. . . . If a man wanted to make an idol and worship it without meddling with his neighbor he should be protected. So that a man should be protected in his rights whether he choose to make a profession of religion or not."[19] The kingdom of God would protect the rights of conscience for Mormons, idolaters, and atheists alike.

JOSEPH SMITH'S VIEWS ON THEODEMOCRACY

Amidst the swirl of theocratic enthusiasm, Joseph Smith emerges in the minutes as perhaps the most moderate member of the council. To be sure, he did allow his colleagues to proclaim him as their prophet, priest, and king.[20] And he was the one who gave Brigham Young the idea that, as chairman of the council, Smith was "a committee of myself."[21] Nevertheless, in the council's discussions of theocracy, Smith left far more room for human agency and coparticipation than did many of his peers. While the word *theodemocracy* is never explicitly used in the minutes by Smith or any other council member, in his remarks on April 11, just four days before publishing the newspaper article that did introduce the term, Smith articulated a vision of God and the people working together to govern human affairs in righteousness. He declared that theocracy meant "exercising all the intelligence of the council, and bringing forth all the light which dwells in the breast of every man, and then let God approve of the document." Smith said it was not only advisable but in fact necessary for the government of the kingdom of God to operate in this fashion so as to prove to the council members that "they are as wise as God himself." A week earlier, Brigham Young had asserted, "The voice of God, shall be the voice of the people," but now Smith reversed that formulation by declaring, "Vox populi, Vox Dei." The people would still assent to the will of God, but in Smith's formulation the process would be far more collaborative than what his colleagues had imagined.[22]

Smith's statements, carving out space for human coparticipation with God, make even more sense when we recognize that they were expressed a mere four days after he delivered his seminal sermon known as the King Follett discourse. In that remarkable address he proclaimed, "God Himself who sits enthroned in yonder heavens is a Man like unto one of yourselves," and further, that the core essence, or intelligence, of each human is "as immortal as, and is coequal with, God Himself."[23] This radical collapse of ontological distance between God and humanity allowed for Smith to believe that humans could confidently speak for and in the name of God—just as he had been doing for nearly two decades. As I concluded in my original article, Joseph Smith's principal impulse was "to bring God and humanity together in radically new ways. . . . Politically, this meant devising a system in which God and the people would work jointly in administering the government of human affairs. The notion of theodemocracy thus represented the logical culmination of Mormon ideas about the social-political relationships that people had with one another and with the divine."[24]

Joseph Smith tempered the more theocratic leanings of his fellow council members not only by introducing *demos* into the equation but also in affirming that the kingdom of God and the church of Jesus Christ were two separate institutions, each with its own laws and jurisdiction. In determining this he was settling a debate that occupied most of the meeting on April 18. "The church is a spiritual matter," he clarified, whereas "the kingdom of God has nothing to do with giving commandments to damn a man spiritually."[25]

DIVERSITY AND DISSENT

Even with this relatively firm understanding of the separation of church and state, Smith and the council never fully grappled with the problem of genuine diversity and dissent. The nature of the council's governance, requiring that all decisions be made with full unanimity, can be interpreted in at least two ways: first, as a pragmatic response to democratic politics intended as a guard against the tyranny of the majority; or second, implying a naive belief that all people of goodwill, especially when guided by the Holy Spirit, would come to the same conclusions on any matter of import. These two interpretations are not mutually exclusive, and both seem plausible when understood against the backdrop of antebellum American politics and culture. Indeed, the second interpretation, with its faith in the very possibility of political and religious consensus, would be consistent with the philosophy regnant in late eighteenth- and early nineteenth-century America which produced "an almost reverential respect for the certainty of knowledge achieved by careful and objective observation of the facts known to common sense."[26] At the time of the Restoration, this "Common Sense philosophy seemed to have swept everything before it in American intellectual life," and virtually "all were convinced that in fair controversy universal truth would eventually flourish."[27] In other words, early nineteenth-century Americans—including Mormons—generally believed that any two or more rational people looking objectively at the same set of facts would come to similar conclusions. Joseph Smith could therefore propose an extreme libertarian view of government, suggesting that "it only requires two or three sentences in a constitution to govern the world," precisely because he believed that equipped with freedom, proper teaching, and correct information, humans could and would act in complete harmony for the common good.[28] The inclusion of three non-Mormons on the council was therefore a gesture not just of tokenism or religious liberality but also an expression of a sincere belief that spiritual difference would not impede social harmony and political unity.

Such sincerity would prove insufficient in the face of real difference and especially dissent. Smith and the other council members, many of whom also served as municipal officials in Nauvoo, were unable to tolerate even a rival newspaper, to say nothing of how their proposed system would respond to the deep pluralism characteristic of modern life in the twenty-first century. All of the council's fine talk of freedom, liberty, and minority rights proved ephemeral when the authority of their prophet, priest, and king was publicly challenged. Whether properly understood as theocracy or theodemocracy, the government of the kingdom of God proved to be incompatible with a pluralistic society and therefore untenable as a modern political theory.[29]

CONCLUSION

The Council of Fifty stands as a fascinating study of the illiberal tradition in American politics and society. Though fueled in substantial part by Smith's millenarian revelations, the theocratic strain in Mormonism must be understood principally as the reaction of a people otherwise inclined toward patriotism and republicanism but deeply scarred by the failure of the American nation to live up to its own highest ideals. Early Mormon theo(demo)cracy can therefore be considered alongside other protest movements born of profound alienation from the American state—such as the American Indian Movement and various black nationalist groups, including the Nation of Islam and Black Panthers. These groups' failure to provide satisfactory alternatives should not diminish our recognition of the potency of their complaints and the depth of their disaffection. In this manner, it is precisely those minority groups who flirt with nondemocratic polities who underscore the nation's perpetual struggle to guarantee, in Joseph Smith's words, "those grand and sublime principles of equal rights and universal freedom to all."[30]

NOTES

1. Joseph Smith, "The Globe," *Times and Seasons* 5, no. 8 (April 15, 1844): 510. The article was ghostwritten by William W. Phelps.

2. Patrick Q. Mason, "God and the People: Theodemocracy in Nineteenth-Century Mormonism," *Journal of Church and State* 53, no. 3 (Summer 2011): 349–75.

3. In his influential 1955 treatise *The Islamic Law and Constitution*, Maududi wrote, "If I were permitted to coin a new term, I would describe this system of government as a 'theo-democracy,' that is to say a divine democratic government, because under it the Muslims have been given a limited popular sovereignty under the suzerainty of God." Sayyid Abul A'la Maududi, *The Islamic Law and Constitution*, trans. and ed. Khurshid Ahmad, 7th ed. (Lahore, Pakistan: Islamic Publications, 1980), 139–40. On the broader context for Maududi's concept of theodemocracy, see Mumtaz Ahmad, "Islamic Fundamentalism in South Asia: The Jamaat-i-Islami and the Tablighi Jamaat of South Asia," in *Fundamentalisms Observed*, ed. Martin E. Marty and Scott Appleby, vol. 1 of *The Fundamentalism Project* (Chicago: University of Chicago Press, 1991), 457–530.

4. An important step in this direction, though still limited to the earliest years of the Mormon movement, is Mark Ashurst-McGee, "Zion Rising: Joseph Smith's Early Social and Political Thought" (PhD diss., Arizona State University, 2008).

5. Mason, "God and the People," 358.

6. Matthew J. Grow, Ronald K. Esplin, Mark Ashurst-McGee, Gerrit J. Dirkmaat, and Jeffrey D. Mahas, eds., *Council of Fifty, Minutes, March 1844–January 1846*, vol. 1 of the Administrative Records series of *The Joseph Smith Papers*, ed. Ronald K. Esplin, Matthew J. Grow, and Matthew C. Godfrey (Salt Lake City: Church Historian's Press, 2016) (hereafter *JSP*, CFM).

7. Mason, "God and the People," 354.

8. Council of Fifty, Minutes, March 19 and April 18, 1844, in *JSP*, CFM:52, 114.

9. Council of Fifty, Minutes, April 11, 1844, in *JSP*, CFM:94; Doctrine and Covenants 101:80.

10. Council of Fifty, Minutes, April 11, 1844, in *JSP*, CFM:104.

11. On Mormonism's optimistic theology, see Terryl Givens and Fiona Givens, *The God Who Weeps: How Mormonism Makes Sense of Life* (Salt Lake City: Ensign Peak, 2012). On early Mormon millenarianism, see Grant Underwood, *The Millenarian World of Early Mormonism* (Urbana: University of Illinois Press, 1993).

12. Council of Fifty, Minutes, March 11, 1844, in *JSP*, CFM:40.

13. Council of Fifty, Minutes, April 11, 1844, in *JSP*, CFM:88.

14. Council of Fifty, Minutes, April 5, 1844, in *JSP*, CFM:82.

15. Council of Fifty, Minutes, April 18, 1844, in *JSP*, CFM:120.

16. See John G. Turner, *Brigham Young: Pioneer Prophet* (Cambridge, MA: Belknap Press of Harvard University Press, 2012); Marianne T. Watson, "The 1948 Secret Marriage of Louis J. Barlow: Origins of FLDS Placement Marriage," *Dialogue: A Journal of Mormon Thought* 40, no. 1 (Spring 2007): 102.

17. Council of Fifty, Minutes, April 4, 1844, in *JSP*, CFM:79.

18. Council of Fifty, Minutes, April 18, 1844, in *JSP*, CFM:112.

19. Council of Fifty, Minutes, April 18, 1844, in *JSP*, CFM:122.

20. Council of Fifty, Minutes, April 11, 1844, in *JSP*, CFM:95–96.

21. Council of Fifty, Minutes, April 11, 1844, in *JSP*, CFM:92.

22. Council of Fifty, Minutes, April 11 and 5, 1844, in *JSP*, CFM:92, 82.

23. Stan Larson, "The King Follett Discourse: A Newly Amalgamated Text," *BYU Studies* 18, no. 2 (1978): 200, 203. Smith's views on religious liberty are also consistent between the April 7 King Follett discourse and his remarks in the Council of Fifty meeting four days later. In the April 7 sermon, he taught, "But meddle not with any man for his religion, for no man is authorized to take away life in consequence of religion. All laws and government ought to tolerate and permit every man to enjoy his religion, whether right or wrong. There is no law in the heart of God that would allow anyone to interfere with the rights of man. Every man has a right to be a false prophet, as well as a true prophet." Larson, "King Follett Discourse," 200. At the April 11 council meeting, he declared, "Nothing can reclaim the human mind from its ignorance, bigotry, superstition &c but those grand and sublime principles of equal rights and universal freedom to all men. . . . Nothing is more congenial to my feelings and principles, than the principles of universal freedom and has been from the beginning. . . . Hence in all governments or political transactions a mans religious opinions should never be called in question. A man should be judged by the law independant of religious prejudice." Council of Fifty, Minutes, April 11, 1844, in *JSP*, CFM:100–101.

24. Mason, "God and the People," 373–74.

25. Council of Fifty, Minutes, April 18, 1844, in *JSP*, CFM:128.

26. George M. Marsden, *Fundamentalism and American Culture: The Shaping of Twentieth-Century Evangelicalism, 1870–1925* (New York: Oxford University Press, 1980), 15; see also Nathan O. Hatch, *The Democratization of American Christianity* (New Haven, CT: Yale University Press, 1989), esp. chaps. 1–2; and James Turner, *Without God, without Creed: The Origins of Unbelief in America* (Baltimore: Johns Hopkins University Press, 1985), 62, 104–9.

27. George M. Marsen, *The Soul of the American University: From Protestant Establishment to Established Nonbelief* (New York: Oxford University Press, 1994), 91.

28. Council of Fifty, Minutes, April 11, 1844, in *JSP*, CFM:101.

29. I explore these problems with theodemocracy at greater length in "God and the People," 363–75.

30. Council of Fifty, Minutes, April 11, 1844, in *JSP*, CFM:100.

Chapter 5

THE COUNCIL OF FIFTY AND THE PERILS OF DEMOCRATIC GOVERNANCE

Benjamin E. Park

The winter of 1843–44 had been exceptionally cold in the Mormon city of Nauvoo, Illinois, and the following spring was especially rainy. The downpour was so strong on April 14 that Joseph Smith, prophet and president of The Church of Jesus Christ of Latter-day Saints, canceled Sunday meetings. Yet despite the gloomy weather, many Mormons' hopes were buoyed by the formation of a new secretive political organization that they believed was destined to rule the world.

Joseph Smith and several dozen of his closest male followers gathered together twice on April 18 in the month-old Council of Fifty, once at 9:00 a.m. and again at 2:00 p.m. During the morning session, they discussed a new document that would take precedence over the American Constitution, which Mormons believed the United States government had abandoned. "We, the people of the Kingdom of God," started the document, which was a mix of traditional republican language with theocratic principles. Though the new constitution was incomplete and required further revision, the delegates enthusiastically praised its general ideas. In the afternoon session, they debated its implications. Throughout, attendees were ecstatic. One participant, Ezra Thayer, remarked that "this [was] the greatest day of his life." William Clayton, the secretary of the council, noted in his journal that "it seems like heaven began on earth and the power of God is with us." The physical setting was wet and dreary, yet the theoretical future seemed anything but.[1]

While part of a seemingly radical fringe response to a particular set of circumstances, the Council of Fifty embodied central American tensions concerning constitutionalism, democratic governance, and the separation between church and state. Understanding the council's relationship to these broader themes is significant in reconstructing not only the turbulent Mormon settlement of Nauvoo but also the dynamic environment of antebellum America. This essay will focus explicitly on the intersections of religious, secular, and constitutional sovereignty and how these intersections were rooted in a culture in which all three spheres seemed to converge. To do so, it will focus on a single day of debates, April 18, 1844, and trace the cultural genealogies found within those discussions. How did the Council of Fifty's radical solutions speak to the problems of democratic governance? The answers promise to add nuance to conventional understanding of America's democratic tradition.

THE KINGDOM OF GOD AND THE CHURCH OF GOD

The afternoon after the Council of Fifty received the first draft of its constitution, Apostle Willard Richards posed two important questions to his fellow council members. One dealt with religious and secular authority, and the other dealt with constitutional evolution. Was there a difference, he asked, between "the kingdom of God and the church of God"? In other words, is there a separation between church and state? While such a question had an immediate and parochial context (would the ecclesiastical and civic structures in Nauvoo overlap?) it also held much broader implications. And reflecting the complex issue, the question prompted a number of divergent, and discursive, responses, and the numerous opinions exemplified the disagreements even within the Church. The second question was even more nuanced. "Will the 'kingdom of God' become perfected as the legitimate results of the operation of the constitution now to be adopted," he asked, "or will it be perfected through the alterations of the constitution which may take place hereafter to suit the situation of

Willard Richards served as recorder of the Council of Fifty during the Nauvoo era. Copy of a photograph, circa 1845, likely by Lucian R. Foster. Courtesy of Church History Library, Salt Lake City.

the earth and kingdom?" Put another way, are the founding documents binding as scripture—a position modern theorists define as originalism— or will governing principles evolve as leaders, generations, and circumstances develop? Few in the council seemed to grasp the significance of this latter question, and discussion soon spiraled out of control. But as we tease out the meanings and contexts of his questions, it becomes apparent that Richards was an acute observer of the democratic dilemma.[2]

Born in Massachusetts and trained in Thomsonian medicine, Richards converted to the Mormon faith in 1836 and became an apostle in 1840. Joseph Smith quickly recognized his able mind and steady hand. Richards was appointed as Joseph Smith's scribe in 1841 and then as Church historian and recorder the following year. He was therefore a natural choice for the Council of Fifty's recorder in 1844. Though William Clayton kept the council's minutes, Richards was a constant presence, mediating voice, and reliable expositor. His questions on April 18, along with his other remarks throughout the council's minutes, reveal him to be a keen observer of key issues. In many ways, his questions were more poignant than even he could have understood at the time.

SEPARATION OF CHURCH AND STATE

Richards's first question, on the difference between the "kingdom" and the "church" of God, reflected how far American society had come in the half century since disestablishment. Those who framed the United States' founding documents inaugurated a then-radical idea of religious liberty— in which there was a strict separation between political and ecclesiastical governance—over the more traditional practice of religious toleration, in which one religious institution would retain preference over others (even if all faiths received some form of liberty). States were slower to adapt to these new policies. Richards's own Massachusetts, for instance, passed a constitution that argued that because "the happiness of a people and the good order and preservation of civil government essentially depend upon piety, religion, and morality," the legislature had the right to establish a state-funded religion "for the support and maintenance of public Protestant teachers of piety, religion, and morality in all cases where such provisions shall not be made voluntarily." Citizens could worship whatever religion they wished, but the state remained committed to the perpetuation of one particular church. Full disestablishment did not reach Massachusetts until 1833, only three years before Richards encountered Mormon missionaries. When Mormon leaders published a statement on government in 1835, it reflected this new understanding: "We do not believe it just to mingle religious influence with civil Government," it declared. That Richards wondered in 1844 whether there was a separation between church and state—when the two institutions were clearly led by the same "prophet, priest, and king"—demonstrated how deep these cultural roots had taken.[3]

But there were still many who wondered if America's disestablishment had gone too far. When the Constitution was being debated, a number of critics pointed to its failure to mention God, the Bible, or religion in general. Evangelicals in the South and Congregationalists in the Northeast insisted that political rights were based on religious principles and that to ignore the role of religion in society risked inviting God's wrath and inaugurating anarchy. During the antebellum period, antislavery and suffragist activists accused America's political system of forgetting its religious past. Women's rights activist Angelina Grimké, for instance, argued that the rules dictated by "the government of God" should take precedence over federal policies that "subjected [women] to the despotic control of man." Abolitionist Theodore Parker similarly argued that American laws must recognize the "absolute Right" dictated by "a moral Law of God," which should serve as the basis for all laws and legislation. Many believed America's morals had become unmoored from the anchor of divine oversight.[4]

The Mormon constitution sought to solve the problem. "None of the nations, kingdoms or governments of the earth do acknowledge the creator of the Universe as their Priest, Lawgiver, King and Sovereign," its preface declared, "neither have they sought unto him for laws by which to govern themselves." The constitution's first article reaffirmed God's supremacy, the second proclaimed the authority of the prophet and priesthood, and the third validated priestly judgment. There was no question where sovereignty should reside. George A. Smith "compared the situation of the world," which did not recognize God's true authority, "to an old ship without a rudder on the midst of the sea." Revelation and divine authority provided the necessary guidance, and the members of the council were willing "to throw out our cable and try to bring the old ship to land." The nautical metaphor emphasized the Council of Fifty's role in providing a saving grace for the rest of the nations. Secular democracy had brought only unrest and war, and only a divine theocracy could reintroduce stability and peace.[5]

Participants in the council that afternoon were divided over what that precisely meant, however, as Richards's inquiry regarding whether there was a difference between "the kingdom of God and the church of God" sparked a lively debate. Reynolds Cahoon could "not see any difference between them," but Amasa Lyman disagreed. "The church has only jurisdiction over its members," Lyman explained, "but the kingdom of God has jurisdiction over all the world." Erastus Snow split the difference by explaining, "They are distinct, one from the other, and yet all identified in one." Clearly, the boundaries were porous and contested. Council members tried to balance their allegiance to prophetic rule and democratic principles. At least four argued there was not a difference between the two entities, and just as many offered countering rejoinders. As much as they tried to reconcile the two spheres, however, their attempts were strained. Exacerbated with the discussion over Joseph Smith's concurrent roles, David Yearsley asked, "How can a man be elected president when he is already proclaimed king[?]" It was a good question.[6]

Joseph Smith, for his part, emphasized there *was* "a distinction between the Church of God and kingdom of God." The political kingdom had authority only in this world and did not play a role in the hereafter. "The church," on the other hand, "is a spiritual matter and a spiritual kingdom." To Joseph Smith, there was a separation between the spiritual and political spheres. A church functioned within the parameters protected by the government, and the temporal "kingdom" would eventually fade away in the Millennium. Further, even though he had earlier been received by the council as a "prophet, priest, and king," Smith downplayed the monarchical language and connotations. "It is not wisdom to use the term 'king,'" he urged. He personally preferred the ambiguous term "theodemocracy," a neologism that captured the blended purposes of theocratic authority and democratic participation. A "theodemocracy," explained Smith in an earlier council meeting, was when "the people . . . get the voice of God and then acknowledge it, and see it executed." The popular American maxim *Vox populi vox Dei* should *not* mean the common translation of "the voice of the people *is* the voice of God" but rather "the voice of the

Joseph Smith emphasized the distinction between the Church and the Council of Fifty. This portrait is believed to be by David Rogers, based on the work of Sutcliffe Maudsley. Courtesy of Church History Museum, Salt Lake City.

people *assenting* to the voice of God." To many outsiders, these would be distinctions without a difference. For Smith and his followers, however, even while the intersections between the Church, the kingdom, and the American government were never fully fleshed out, the resulting ambiguity enabled a space for creative innovation and theorizing.[7]

THE NATURE OF CONSTITUTIONS

But while they debated the first of Richards's questions on April 18, members of the Council of Fifty failed to address his second query: "Will the 'kingdom of God' become perfected as the legitimate results of the operation of the constitution now to be adopted, or will it be perfected through the alterations of the constitution which may take place hereafter to suit the situation of the earth and kingdom?" Was this new constitution pristine in its original form, or will it have to be adapted as the kingdom, and society, advances? This seemingly abstract and theoretical question regarding originalism reflected a much broader American anxiety: What happens when founding documents fail to definitively answer pressing questions? In an era when the entire nation debated how to address the slave issue—what many saw as the "original sin" of the Constitution—theories concerning origins, alterations, and advancements were abundant.[8]

The late eighteenth and early nineteenth centuries witnessed an intellectual revolution regarding social evolution. Rather than staid institutions frozen in place, nations and governments were now understood to be organic and malleable structures that transformed with time and culture. The American Revolution inaugurated a new age in which the living had the right, even the obligation, to reform the works of the dead. "No society can make a perpetual constitution, or even a perpetual law," declared Thomas Jefferson. "The earth belongs always to the living generation." Jefferson's belief concerning the permanence of government—he argued that "every constitution, and every law, naturally expires at the end of 19 years"—may have been extreme, but it was the product of a cultural environment no longer tethered to traditional forms of authority. In a world in which everything seemed in flux, it made sense to forgo installing permanent shackles.[9]

This anxiety only grew during the antebellum period, as antislavery theorists like William Lloyd Garrison and Wendell Phillips argued that existing governing mechanisms, even if they were enshrined in constitutional law, were not set in stone. When faced with the dilemma of America's founding document being defined as a slaveholding compact, Garrison responded by "branding [the Constitution] a covenant with death, and an agreement with hell" and then burning it before an eager abolitionist audience. Representing a more moderate perspective, Abraham Lincoln argued that founding documents contained the "natural rights" owed to all men but that the governing texts must be amended to better secure those rights. Adapting the Constitution to natural rights was the work of the present. In all corners, the legal foundations upon which Americans placed political authority appeared in transition. Willard Richards's question regarding originalism, then, tapped into a larger ideological debate.[10]

Even if Richards's query went unanswered on April 18, it did not remain so for long. A week later, Smith recorded a revelation declaring that the entire *council* was "my constitution, and I am your God, and ye are my spokesmen." A document could never supplant an authoritative body of chosen men. Divine law was so fluid, and human society so malleable, that constant deliberation was required. This was a culmination of nearly two decades' worth of ecclesiastical development within the Church, as councils were given increasing authority and attention. To Smith, varying contexts and circumstances necessitated holy men who could appropriate ideas and practices as situations required. The constitutional tradition within the Mormon faith, therefore, was closer to the British approach of an unwritten constitution of laws and legislation than it was to the American system of authoritative founding documents. The Council of Fifty's members were eager to receive this course correction. Apostle and prolific author Parley Pratt, who was one of the authors of the draft constitution, noted that he "burnt [his] scribbling" as soon as "a ray of light shewed" that the council was to be the constitution itself. The voice of God's chosen people was the voice of God.[11]

This delicate balance would soon be tested by both internal personalities and external pressures. Most notably, Brigham Young was not as interested in squaring prophetic counsel with populist governance. At the same April 18 meeting, Young declared that it wouldn't matter if "the whole church" disagreed with Smith, because Smith "is a perfect committee of himself." The core democratic principle of compromise was misguided because it hindered progress and qualified God's rule. Young could not conceive of a "difference between a religious or political government," as the prophetic authority in the former also wielded control in the latter. This emphasis became only more apparent when Young took control of the council after Smith's death. In April 1845, Young declared that he would "defy any man to draw the line between the spiritual and temporal affairs in the kingdom of God." His fellow leaders took notice. Correctly reading the chasm between Mormons and their Illinois neighbors, William Phelps posited that "the greatest fears manifested by our enemies is the union of Church and State." Yet Phelps was fine with this accusation: "I believe we are actually doing this and it is what the Lord designs." Young, Phelps, and other Mormons were willing to embrace a principle theoretically alien to the American experiment. The martyrdom of their prophet left them wanting to turn back the errors of disestablishment in total.[12]

CONCLUSION

The Council of Fifty was, in an important way, a direct response to two issues central to American political culture, which were aptly embodied in Willard Richards's two questions: What is the proper relationship between church and state? And how should a government evolve in response to the circumstances in which it governs? The Mormon answers to these questions were, admittedly, radical (not to mention short lived). The Church adopted America's system of democratic governance by the twentieth century, and Mormons are seen as some of the biggest defenders of that tradition today. But in 1844, no solution to the problem of democratic rule appeared definitive. Within two decades, the nation would go to war over the issue of political sovereignty. And in many respects, the same questions posed by Richards remain precariously unanswered even today. So even if the Council of Fifty does not provide resolutions that are relevant for the twenty-first century, the anxieties from which they were birthed are anything but irrelevant.

NOTES

1. Council of Fifty, Minutes, April 18, 1844, in Matthew J. Grow, Ronald K. Esplin, Mark Ashurst-McGee, Gerrit J. Dirkmaat, and Jeffrey D. Mahas, eds., *Council of Fifty, Minutes, March 1844–January 1846,* vol. 1 of the Administrative Records series of *The Joseph Smith Papers,* ed. Ronald K. Esplin, Matthew J. Grow, and Matthew C. Godfrey (Salt Lake City: Church Historian's Press, 2016), 108–10

(hereafter *JSP*, CFM); William Clayton, Journal, April 18, 1844, in *An Intimate Chronicle: The Journals of William Clayton*, ed. George D. Smith (Salt Lake City: Signature Books, 1995), 131. The rained-out Sunday meeting is mentioned in Joseph Smith, Journal, April 14, 1844, in Andrew H. Hedges, Alex D. Smith, and Brent M. Rogers, eds., *Journals, Volume 3: May 1843–June 1844*, vol. 3 of the Journals series of *The Joseph Smith Papers*, ed. Ronald K. Esplin and Matthew J. Grow (Salt Lake City: Church Historian's Press, 2015), 230. The cold winter is described in William Mosley to Kingsley Mosley, February 18, 1844, Church History Library, Salt Lake City. The rainy spring is mentioned in Robert A. Gilmore to John Richey, July 5, 1844, Church History Library.

2. Council of Fifty, Minutes, April 18, 1844, in *JSP*, CFM:121–22.

3. Constitution of the Commonwealth of Massachusetts, part 1, art. III, https://malegislature.gov/Laws/Constitution; "Of Governments and Laws in General," *Doctrine and Covenants of the Church of the Latter Day Saints*, comp. Joseph Smith Jr. et al. (Kirtland, OH: F. G. Williams, 1835), 253 (modern Doctrine and Covenants 134:9); Council of Fifty, Minutes, April 11, 1844, in *JSP*, CFM:95–96.

4. Angelina Emily Grimké, "Letter XII: Human Rights Not Founded on Sex," in Angelina Emily Grimké, *Letters to Catherine E. Beecher: In Reply to an Essay on Slavery and Abolitionism, Addressed to A. E. Grimke, Revised by the Author* (Boston: Isaac Knapp, 1838), 115; Theodore Parker, "National Sins," Sermon Book 10:421, Theodore Parker Collection, Andover-Harvard Theological Library, Harvard Divinity School, Cambridge, MA. For the religious critique of the Constitution, see Joseph S. Moore, *Founding Sins: How a Group of Antislavery Radicals Fought to Put Christ into the Constitution* (New York: Oxford University Press, 2015); and Spencer W. McBride, *Pulpit and Nation: Clergymen and the Politics of Revolutionary America* (Charlottesville: University of Virginia Press, 2017).

5. Council of Fifty, Minutes, April 18, 1844, in *JSP*, CFM:110–15.

6. Council of Fifty, Minutes, April 18, 1844, in *JSP*, CFM:121–25.

7. Council of Fifty, Minutes, April 11 and 18, 1844, in *JSP*, CFM:92, 95–96, 121–22, 128, emphasis added; see also Patrick Q. Mason, "God and the People: Theodemocracy in Nineteenth-Century Mormonism," *Journal of Church and State* 53, no. 3 (Summer 2011): 349–75.

8. Council of Fifty, Minutes, April 18, 1844, in *JSP*, CFM:122. For this context, see Jordan T. Watkins, "Slavery, Sacred Texts, and the Antebellum Confrontation with History" (PhD diss., University of Nevada, Las Vegas, 2014).

9. Thomas Jefferson to James Madison, September 6, 1789, in *The Portable Thomas Jefferson*, ed. Merrill D. Peterson (New York: Penguin, 1975), 449; see Eric Slauter, *The State as a Work of Art: The Cultural Origins of the Constitution* (Chicago: University of Chicago Press, 2010); and Benjamin E. Park, "The Bonds of Union: Benjamin Rush, Noah Webster, and Defining the Nation in the Early Republic," *Early American Studies* 15, no. 2 (Spring 2017).

10. "The Meeting at Framingham," *Liberator*, July 7, 1854; Abraham Lincoln, Speech, August 21, 1858, in *Lincoln: Speeches, Letters, Miscellaneous Writings*, vol. 1, *The Lincoln-Douglas Debates*, ed. Don E. Fehrenbacher (New York: Modern Library, 1984), 512. For Garrison's constitutional views, see W. Caleb McDaniel, *The Problem of Democracy in the Age of Slavery: Garrisonian Abolitionists and Transatlantic Reform* (Baton Rouge: Louisiana State University Press, 2013); for Lincoln's, see John Burt, *Lincoln's Tragic Pragmatism: Lincoln, Douglas, and Moral Conflict* (Cambridge: Harvard University Press, 2012).

11. Council of Fifty, Minutes, April 25, 1844, in *JSP*, CFM:137; Pratt is quoted in *JSP*, CFM:137n412; see Richard Lyman Bushman, "Joseph Smith and Power," in *A Firm Foundation: Church Organization and Administration*, ed. David J. Whittaker and Arnold K. Garr (Provo, UT: Religious Studies Center, 2011), 1–13; and Kathleen Flake, "Ordering Antinomy: An Analysis of Early Mormonism's Priestly Offices, Councils, and Kinship," *Religion and American Culture* 26, no. 2 (Summer 2016): 139–83.

12. Council of Fifty, Minutes, April 18, 1844; March 4, 1845; April 11, 1845, in *JSP*, CFM:119–20, 285, 401.

Chapter 6

"WE, THE PEOPLE OF THE KINGDOM OF GOD"

Constitution Writing in the Council of Fifty

Nathan B. Oman

In the spring of 1844, Joseph Smith created a secret organization, the Council of Fifty, of high church officials, civic leaders, and others, and tasked it with establishing the kingdom of God, a political organization to be set up by the Mormons someplace on the North American continent in expectation of the imminent end times. This grandiose goal came amid very concrete concerns about the deteriorating political situation in Illinois and the felt need for the Mormons to look elsewhere for a place of refuge. Once operating, the Council of Fifty spent the lion's share of its efforts on the practical questions of where to locate the projected Mormon commonwealth and how to escape from hostile neighbors and governments. On March 11, 1844, however, the council appointed a committee of John Taylor, Willard Richards, William W. Phelps, and Parley P. Pratt "to draft a constitution which should be perfect, and embrace those principles of which the constitution of the United States lacked."[1] Slightly more than a month later, on April 18, the committee reported a draft constitution to the entire council. The authors, however, expressed their dissatisfaction with their work, and it was returned to committee.[2] A week later, Joseph Smith announced to the council a revelation abandoning the effort to draft a written constitution for the kingdom of God, and the council devoted

On April 25, 1844, Joseph Smith announced a revelation that brought to an end the Council of Fifty's efforts to draft a constitution for the council. Painting by David Rogers, 1842. Courtesy of Community of Christ Library-Archives, Independence, Missouri.

the rest of its efforts to the more immediate problems facing the Saints, culminating in the relocation en masse of the Mormons to the Great Basin after Joseph Smith's murder.[3]

This bare statement of events casts the Mormons as radicals, operating scandalously outside the American political tradition.[4] The Treaty of Paris, which ended the American Revolution, placed the western border of the United States on the Mississippi River. Beginning with the Northwest Ordinance of 1785, Congress organized the area west of the Appalachian Mountains into discrete territories, with local governments under federal supervision. In time, these territories became states. With the exception of the unsuccessful effort to conquer Canada in the War of 1812, this orderly process of expansion continued as the United States government trans-formed the Louisiana Purchase and the cession from Mexico into terri-tories and then states. Thus the United States established itself as a single polity occupying the center of North America. Within this narrative of unified national expansion at the expense of native tribes, Spain, France, and Mexico, the Mormon dream of an independent commonwealth and an alternative constitution is a jarring aberration.

AN AMERICAN HISTORY OF BREAKAWAY REPUBLICS

The problem is that the narrative of smooth national expansion is false. In the nineteenth century, North America was littered with abortive republics seeking varying levels of independence from the federal gov-ernment and from the other competing powers on the continent. Very early in the history of the United States, settlers formed break-away pol-ities on the borders of existing states. Vermont, for example, declared itself an independent republic before being incorporated as a state in 1791. The abortive State of Franklin, which would have sat athwart the Blue Ridge and Appalachian Mountains, was less successful.[5] In 1804, Aaron Burr—Thomas Jefferson's disgruntled vice president—began hatch-ing plans to detach the western territories of the United States to form a new nation with himself at its head. Those efforts ended in failure when a co-conspirator betrayed him to Jefferson in 1806.[6] In 1810, American set-tlers in Spanish territory declared the Republic of West Florida, raising the lone star flag that would be adopted by Texas revolutionaries a few decades later. In the 1830s, as the Mormon movement gathered steam, settlers in the disputed borderlands between Canada and the United States declared the tiny Indian Stream Republic.[7] More spectacularly, American filibusters in Mexico managed to detach the territory north and east of the Rio Grande to form the Republic of Texas, which operated as an independent nation from 1836 to 1846.[8] Shortly after the Council of Fifty adjourned its meetings in Nauvoo for the last time, American settlers in the Mexican province of Upper California declared the short-lived Bear Flag Republic.[9] As late as 1894, American businessmen in the Sandwich Islands formed the Republic of Hawaii, which operated as an independent nation for four years. Most dramatically, the Confederate States of America made a bid for political independence from 1861 to 1865.

It is only against this far messier background of American political history that we can see what was unique in the abortive constitution making of the Council of Fifty in March and April of 1844. The urge to found a new republic in the liminal spaces of the continent and author a new constitution for it was not unique. Rather, Mormons stood firmly within an American tradition running from Aaron Burr to Sam Houston. They were not even unique in injecting religion into their constitution writing. John Brown's proposed constitution for a redeemed America spoke in apocalyptic religious terms, and the constitutional preamble beginning "We, the people of the Confederate States" invoked "the favor and guidance of Almighty God."[10] Rather, what is striking is that in their constitution making, the Mormons ultimately turned away from written constitutionalism.

THE US CONSTITUTION IN MORMON SCRIPTURE

Contemporary Mormons often affirm that their scriptures teach about "the divinely inspired constitution" of the United States.[11] However, the revelations of Joseph Smith do not contain this exact phrase. The Constitution makes its first appearance in those revelations in August 1833.[12] The worsening affairs in Missouri seem to have been on Joseph Smith's mind when he dictated a revelation in which the Lord stated: "And that law of the land which is constitutional, supporting that principle of freedom in maintaining rights and privileges, belongs to all mankind, and is justifiable before me. . . . Nevertheless, when the wicked rule the people mourn.

Wherefore, honest men and wise men should be sought for diligently, and good men and wise men ye should observe to uphold; otherwise whatsoever is less than these cometh of evil" (D&C 98:5, 9–10).

A few months later, having heard the details of the increasingly intense pressure on Mormons in Missouri, Joseph dictated a second revelation, in which the Lord said: "Therefore, it is not right that any man should be in bondage one to another. And for this purpose have I established the Constitution of this land, by the hands of wise men whom I raised up unto this very purpose, and redeemed the land by the shedding of blood" (D&C 101:79–80). These revelations represent the appearance of the US Constitution in the revelations of Joseph Smith, which had previously spoken only of God's law.

From a constitutional perspective, the most striking thing about these passages is how ordinary they are by the standards of the time. The idea that the US Constitution embodied general principles of freedom and justice was widely accepted. Likewise, the providential role of God in the American founding was a commonplace. The revelations also presented a conservative and even anachronistic vision of politics. American politics today could be called a procedural republic, a system where the public interest is supposed to emerge from competition between interest groups pursuing narrow agendas within the context of a supposedly neutral constitutional order.[13] Joseph Smith's revelations, however, did not present the US Constitution in these familiar modern terms. Rather, they presented politics as essentially adjudicative, with "honest men and wise men" (D&C 98:10) and "wise men whom I raised up unto this very purpose" (D&C 101:80) applying the "principle of freedom in maintaining rights and privileges" (D&C 98:5) as "rulers of our land" (D&C 109:54). This vision is republican and aristocratic, focusing on wise statesmen above party or faction. Absent is any valorization of democracy or the common man. In Joseph Smith's revelations, vox populi is not vox dei; that is, the voice of the people is not the voice of God. Rather, the ideal is of virtuous leaders, what John Adams called a "natural Aristocracy of 'Virtues and Talents,'"[14] disinterestedly applying timeless principles. In this, Joseph Smith's early constitutional revelations hark back to the republican tradition that, in part, animated early American politics.[15] Crucially, for this adjudicative model of statesmanship, the emergence of organized political parties and mass political movements was problematic. While political parties were well established by Joseph Smith's time, they remained disconcerting for many nineteenth-century Americans.[16] It was difficult for many Americans to see such politics as anything other than a fall from a more noble past into a grubby and amoral tournament of selfish factions.

A CONSTITUTION FOR THE KINGDOM OF GOD

By 1840, Mormon faith in this constitutional model had been shattered. Events in Missouri had played themselves out to their bitter conclusion, with the expulsion first from Jackson County and then from the entire state. Mormon property had been seized, Mormons had been massacred by mobs, Mormon women had been raped, and Governor Lilburn Boggs had issued his extermination order. Efforts at relief before the courts of Missouri were futile. Finally, Joseph Smith traveled to Washington, DC, to petition the nation's statesmen for relief. There he ran up against the realities of antebellum federalism and the electoral needs of Martin Van Buren's embattled Democratic Party.[17] That disjunction proved decisive for the political development of Mormonism. No relief for the Mormons was forthcoming from the federal government. In the end the federal Constitution was wholly inadequate as a mechanism for protecting Mormon rights, and in Mormon eyes "honest men and wise men" were nowhere to be seen in high office. It was in this context of deepening disillusionment toward the United States and its legal institutions that the Council of Fifty embarked on its constitution-making project.

There are two features of the text presented by Taylor, Richards, Phelps, and Pratt that are immediately apparent. The first is that unlike most efforts at American constitution making, the document was written without copying from an existing constitution. There are, to be sure, echoes of the federal Constitution in its basic structure. The document begins with a preamble announcing its authors as "We, the people of the Kingdom of God"[18] and is divided into articles like the Constitution of 1787. However, there is no copying of governing structure or text from that Constitution or any other. As the committee explained, in writing the document "they cant refer to any constitution of the world because they are corrupt."[19] The second feature is that the constitution is in no sense a practical document. Only in the final article is there any effort to articulate procedures or institutions for governing a community, and then only in the most skeletal form. In this sense, it is perhaps closer in genre to the Declaration of Independence, which propounded a theory of just government, as opposed to the Constitution of 1787, which contained elaborate rules on such eminently practical subjects as taxation and the spending of government money. As written, the constitution of the kingdom of God was less an effort to construct a working legal system than to set forth a theory of government.

Roughly half of the document consisted of a prolonged preamble condemning all contemporary political arrangements. The preamble concludes:

> We have supplicated the great I am, that he would make known his will unto his servants, concerning this, his last kingdom, and the law, by which his people shall be governed: And the voice of the Lord unto us was,— Verily thus saith the Lord, this is the name by which you shall be called, the kingdom of God and his Laws, with the keys and power thereof, and Judgement in the hands of his servants, Ahman Christ.[20]

The second half of the document consists of three articles in which "I . . . the Lord thy God" rather than "We, the people of the Kingdom of God" speaks in the first person. The constitution thus aspires to be a direct revelation from God, consistent with the claim in the preamble that "the supreme law of the land shall be the word of Jehovah,"[21] a stark and perhaps deliberate contrast to article 6 of the US Constitution, which declares that the "supreme Law of the Land" shall be the constitution, laws, and treaties of the United States.[22]

The critique of existing governments begins with the assertion of the sovereignty of God. "All power emanates from God, . . . and he alone has the right to govern the nations and set in order the kingdoms of this world."[23] The "We, the people" of this document is thus fundamentally different than the "We the People" of the constitution of 1787, who claimed themselves as a sufficient font of sovereignty. Mormon political thinking on the nature of sovereignty had already begun moving in this direction nearly a decade earlier, when the Church's 1835 declaration of beliefs regarding governments stated, "We believe that governments were instituted of God" (D&C 134:1), implicitly rejecting the idea that governments are established by the consent of the governed.[24] By 1844, however, Taylor, Richards, Phelps, and Pratt were prepared to state categorically that all existing governments were illegitimate because "none of the nations, kingdoms or governments of the earth do acknowledge the <u>creator</u> of the <u>Universe</u> as their Priest, Lawgiver, King and Sovereign, neither have they sought unto him for laws by which to govern themselves." Rather "all the nations have obtained their power, rule and authority by usurpation, rebellion, bloodshed, tyranny and fraud."[25] This is a Hobbesian vision of the state unredeemed even by Hobbes's Leviathan.[26]

The preamble also invoked mainstays of American political thought: the rights of man and utility. Because existing governments arise from "usurpation, rebellion, bloodshed, tyranny and fraud," they lack "the disposition and power to grant that protection to the persons and rights of man, viz. <u>life</u>, <u>liberty</u>, <u>possession</u> of <u>property</u>, and <u>pursuit</u> of <u>happiness</u>, which was designed by their creator to all men." The debt to the Declaration of Independence's vision of men "endowed by their Creator with certain unalienable Rights, that among these are Life, Liberty and the pursuit of Happiness" is clear. The usurpations of human governments also result in human suffering. The preamble declares that "the natural results of these illegitimate governments" are "cruelty, oppression, bondage, slavery, rapine, bloodshed, murder, carnage, desolation, and all the evils that blast the peace, exaltation, and glory of the universe." From the cosmic "glory of the universe," the preamble descends to what was no doubt a description of contemporary American politics from the Mormon point of view, insisting that by ignoring God, governments have bred "pride, corruption, impurity, intrigue, spiritual wickedness in high places, party spirit, faction, perplexity and distress of nations."[27] This is the voice of those whose hopes of a political order in the "hands of wise men whom [the Lord] raised up unto this very purpose" (D&C 101:80) had been dashed on the realities of party and regional politics in democratic America. In response to this disappointment, the voice of the Lord in the three articles of the constitution presents an even more extreme version of this vision of adjudicative politics.

In article 1, the Lord announces that he rules "the armies of heaven above, and among the nations of the earth beneath." He insists that "I alone am the rightful lawgiver to man."[28] Intentionally or unintentionally, this claim mirrors the structure of the US Constitution, where article 1 also begins with the law-making power, declaring in contrast that "all legislative powers herein granted shall be vested in a Congress of the United States, which shall consist of a Senate and House of Representatives."[29] In article 2, "wise men raised up for this very purpose" are replaced with even more inspired agents of God's providence:

> I the Lord will do nothing but what I have revealed or shall reveal unto my servants the prophets and I have appointed one man, holding the keys and authority, pertaining to my holy priesthood, to whom I will reveal my laws, my statutes, my ordinances, my Judgements, my will and pleasure concerning my kingdom on the earth.[30]

Wise statesmen adjudicating the public good have been replaced by an inspired prophet announcing God's designs.[31] Both sit above the "pride, corruption, impurity, intrigue, spiritual wickedness in high places, party spirit, [and] faction" of a corrupt democracy. In the Council of Fifty, however, the aristocracy of republican virtue is transformed into the spiritual aristocracy of priestly and prophetic authority. Only in article 3, the single vast final sentence of the document, do we find anything that resembles the ordinary subject of written constitutions, namely governing procedures. "My Servant and Prophet whom I have called and chosen shall have power to appoint Judges and officers in my kingdom, And my people shall have the right to choose or refuse those officers and judges, by common consent. . . . And if the judges or officers transgress, they shall be punished according to my laws."[32] This is also the only place in the constitution in which the will of the people is given any play in the vision of the kingdom of God. It is an attempt to find a place for democracy in a political vision that ultimately rejects the idea of popular sovereignty. The model was clearly the emerging ecclesiology of the Church, in which members were asked to give their assent and support to the revelations of the leadership.[33]

Taken as a whole, the constitution of the kingdom of God is less a blueprint for a functioning government than an effort to state a philosophy of government. At its center is the absolute sovereignty of God. Acknowledging that sovereignty and following God's laws will lead to the protection of rights to life, liberty, property, and the pursuit of happiness. Disregarding God's sovereignty leads to misery and suffering. In a properly functioning polity, the community is led by benevolent and inspired leaders endowed with divine authority and upheld by the common consent of the people. As to whether their draft was a revelation, however, the authors of the constitution of the kingdom of God expressed their doubts. Upon reporting the committee's work to the council, John Taylor said, "If they can get intelligence from God they can write correct principles, if not, they cannot."[34] But he did not claim that the committee had in fact found that inspiration. They were sent back to work, presumably to search for more "intelligence from God." Parley P. Pratt later gave a hint as to the problem faced by the committee. "If we made a constitution it would be a man made thing, and he considered that if God gave us laws to govern us and we received those laws God must also give us a constitution."[35] It wasn't enough to state a proper theory of government or announce wise legal mechanisms. As the first-person voice of the Lord in articles 1 through 3 testified, the committee believed that they must produce a revelation, something that they did not seem to feel they had done.[36]

THE ABANDONMENT OF CONSTITUTION WRITING

They were never allowed, however, to complete their work. Rather, in late April Joseph Smith "advised that we let the constitution alone."[37] He summed up the "whole matter about the constitution" in a three-sentence revelation:

> Verily thus saith the Lord, ye are my constitution, and I am your God, and ye are my spokesmen. From henceforth do as I shall command you. Saith the Lord.[38]

The revelation ended any further discussion of a written constitution for the kingdom of God. Rather, the council simply abandoned the project and focused its attention on the immediate practical concerns facing the Saints, including their ongoing legal difficulties. They certainly did not abandon the ideal of a political kingdom of God, and they pursued often fanciful plans, such as massive military alliances with American Indian tribes. In that sense, the revelation did not represent any turning away from theocratic ambitions.

Almost exactly two months after reporting his revelation to the Council of Fifty, Joseph Smith was murdered. The April document is the final constitutional statement in Joseph Smith's revelations. As noted above, Joseph's revelations of a decade earlier present a thoroughly conventional political theology in which the federal constitution embodies principles of justice and freedom to be upheld by wise and honest rulers. It is an aristocratic and republican vision rather than a liberal or a democratic one, but it fit within the mainstream of American political thought, albeit in a way that was increasingly anachronistic even when the revelation was given. The adjudicative ideal of republican politics had given way by the 1840s to mass political parties and a politics based on a balancing of sectional interests. Joseph's revelation to the Council of Fifty, however, seems to have finally escaped the gravitational force of American constitutional models. In place of a written document setting forth the formal procedures of government, the sine qua non of American constitution making, the revelation offered an existing body of men endowed with divine authority as all the constitutional structure that was necessary for the kingdom of God.

In September 1897, George Q. Cannon, then an aging counselor in the First Presidency of the Church, spoke at a church conference in Paris, Idaho. Less than a decade earlier, in 1890, President Wilford Woodruff had issued the Manifesto, publicly abandoning plural marriage, bringing the federal government's legal crusade against the Mormons to an end. Just the year before Cannon's sermon, Utah had been formally admitted to the Union as a state. While the Mormon conflict with the nation would dramatically flare up one final time a few years later during the Smoot hearings, Mormonism's theocratic ambitions were at an end, and the political kingdom of God had been postponed to an ever-delayed millennium.[39]

Strikingly, however, Cannon chose to preach on Joseph Smith's April 1844 revelation to the Council of Fifty:

> There was an attempt made . . . during the life of Joseph Smith, by some of the priesthood, at the prophet's request, to write a constitution for the kingdom of God. A committee was appointed of the most capable men. They tried and tried to draft it, and so did the prophet himself, but all in vain. Joseph sought the Lord, and he told him: "Ye are the constitution of my church." And so it is; the priesthood, the living oracles, are the word of God unto us, and this constitutes the growth and strength of the kingdom of God.[40]

Cannon's subtle recasting of the precise language of the revelation is telling. Joseph Smith's original "Ye are my constitution" becomes "Ye are the constitution of my church." It is a shift that marks the final afterlife of the prophet's final revelation on the constitution.

CONCLUSION

Scholars have noted the way in which Mormons after 1890 exchanged theocratic ideas for a vision of Church government where, ideally, righteous and inspired leaders upheld by the consent of members would lead the community in its religious—if not its political—life.[41] The ability of Mormon thinkers in the early twentieth century, such as Orson F. Whitney and James E. Talmage, to make this move was important in creating continuity within Mormon religious discourse even as Mormon political, social, and religious ambitions were radically transformed. This flexibility, which somehow managed to treasure the Mormon experience even as much of it was being repudiated, helped Mormonism to survive and, in many ways, thrive in the modern world. In some sense, this too is a legacy of Joseph Smith's April 1844 revelation. Had the kingdom of God been poured into an inspired written constitution as originally envisioned by Taylor, Richards, Phelps, and Pratt, it would almost certainly have shattered amid the legal battles with the federal government over the "Mormon Question" after the Civil War. The fluid, unwritten structure bequeathed to the kingdom of God by Joseph Smith, however, proved more resilient.

To be sure, nineteenth-century Mormon theologians drew careful—if not always consistent—distinctions between church and kingdom, the Council of Fifty and the Church of Jesus Christ of Latter-day Saints.[42] Still, "ye are my constitution, and I am your God, and ye are my spokesmen" is a constitutional ideal easily taken up in a church populated by prophets and apostles. By shifting theocratic ideas from the political kingdom of God to the ecclesiastical structure of the Church, Cannon and those that followed him could reach back to Joseph Smith's earliest revelations on the US Constitution without the later constitutional complications of the Council of Fifty.[43] It is a constitutional vision that allows contemporary Latter-day Saints to make their peace with human governments and continue to build up the kingdom of God, albeit in radically different ways than their nineteenth-century forebears attempted.

NOTES

1. Council of Fifty, Minutes, March 19, 1844, in Matthew J. Grow, Ronald K. Esplin, Mark Ashurst-McGee, Gerrit J. Dirkmaat, and Jeffrey D. Mahas, eds., *Council of Fifty, Minutes, March 1844–January 1846*, vol. 1 of the Administrative Records series of *The Joseph Smith Papers*, ed. Ronald K. Esplin, Matthew J. Grow, and Matthew C. Godfrey (Salt Lake City: Church Historian's Press, 2016), 54 (hereafter *JSP*, CFM).

2. Council of Fifty, Minutes, April 18, 1844, in *JSP*, CFM:110–15.

3. Council of Fifty, Minutes, April 25, 1844, in *JSP*, CFM:135–37.

4. See, for example, Grant H. Palmer, "Did Joseph Smith Commit Treason in His Quest for Political Empire in 1844?" *John Whitmer Historical Association Journal* 32, no. 2 (2012): 52–58.

5. Echoes of the lost State of Franklin continued to reverberate as late as the Civil War, when east Tennessee supported the Union and attempted to secede from the Confederacy. See Eric Foner, *Reconstruction: America's Unfinished Revolution, 1863–1877* (New York: Harper & Row, 1988), 62.

6. Burr said so many different things to so many different people about his plans that it is difficult to determine his ultimate goals. See Gordon S. Wood, *Empire of Liberty: A History of the Early Republic, 1789–1815*, The Oxford History of the United States (New York: Oxford University Press, 2009), 384–85.

7. See Robert L. Tsai, *America's Forgotten Constitutions* (Cambridge, MA: Harvard University Press, 2014), 18–48.

8. See Michael Van Wagenen, *The Texas Republic and the Mormon Kingdom of God*, South Texas Regional Studies, no. 2 (College Station: Texas A&M University Press, 2002).

9. See John A. Hawgood, "John C. Frémont and the Bear Flag Revolution: A Reappraisal," *Southern California Quarterly* 44, no. 2 (1962): 67–96; George Tays, "California Never Was an Independent Republic," *California Historical Society Quarterly* 15, no. 3 (1936): 242–43.

10. See Tsai, *America's Forgotten Constitutions*, 83–117; "Constitution of the Confederate States, March 11, 1861," *The Avalon Project, Yale Law School*, http://avalon.law.yale.edu/19th_century/csa_csa.asp.

11. See, for example, Dallin H. Oaks, "The Divinely Inspired Constitution," *Ensign*, February 1992, 68–74.

12. See Mark Ashurst-McGee, "Zion in America: The Origins of Mormon Constitutionalism," *Journal of Mormon History* 38, no. 3 (2012): 90–101.

13. See V. O. Key, *Politics, Parties, & Pressure Groups*, 5th ed. (New York: Crowell, 1964); Richard Hofstadter, *The American Political Tradition: And the Men Who Made It*, reissue ed. (New York: Vintage, 1989). Louis Menand identifies the intellectual origins of this vision in the American pragmatist tradition, which emerged after the Civil War. See Louis Menand, *The Metaphysical Club: A Story of Ideas in America*, Reprint ed. (New York: Farrar, Straus and Giroux, 2002). However, one can find intimations of it, if one is so inclined, as early as *Federalist* No. 10. See Alexander Hamilton, John Jay, and James Madison, *The Federalist: A Commentary on the Constitution of the United States*, ed. Robert Scigliano (New York: Modern Library, 2001), no. 10 (Madison).

14. Thomas Jefferson and John Adams, *The Adams-Jefferson Letters*, ed. Lester J. Cappon (Chapel Hill: University of North Carolina Press and the Omohundro Institute of Early American History and Culture, 1988), 400.

15. See Gordon S. Wood, *The Creation of the American Republic, 1776–1787* (Chapel Hill: Published for the Institute of Early American History and Culture at Williamsburg Va. by the University of North Carolina Press, 1998).

16. Compare Wood, *Empire of Liberty*, 34–35. While dated, see also Richard Hofstadter, *The Idea of a Party System: The Rise of Legitimate Opposition in the United States, 1780–1840* (Berkeley: University of California Press, 1970). This work traces the historical processes in thought by which American political

leaders slowly edged away from their complete philosophical rejection of a party and hesitantly began to embrace a party system. In the author's words, "The emergence of legitimate party opposition and of a theory of politics that accepted it was something new in the history of the world; it required a bold new act of understanding on the part of its contemporaries and it still requires study on our part." Professor Hofstadter's analysis of the idea of party and the development of legitimate opposition offers fresh insights into the political crisis of 1797–1801, on the thought of George Washington, Thomas Jefferson, James Madison, James Monroe, Martin Van Buren, and other leading figures, and on the beginnings of modern democratic politics."

17. See Ronald O. Barney, "Joseph Smith Goes to Washington," in *Joseph Smith, the Prophet and Seer*, ed. Richard Neitzel Holzapfel and Kent P. Jackson (Provo, UT: Religious Studies Center; Salt Lake City: Deseret Book, 2010), 391–420. Indeed, there is an almost perfect symmetry in the fact that Joseph Smith came to Washington based on a vision of adjudicative politics by a natural aristocracy to meet Van Buren, who wrote one of the first analyses and defenses of mass political parties in American history. See Martin Van Buren, *Inquiry into the Origin and Course of Political Parties in the United States*, ed. Abraham Van Buren and John Van Buren (New York: Hurd and Houghton, 1867).

18. Council of Fifty, Minutes, April 18, 1844, in *JSP*, CFM:110.

19. Council of Fifty, Minutes, April 18, 1844, in *JSP*, CFM:114.

20. Council of Fifty, Minutes, April 18, 1844, in *JSP*, CFM:112–13, underlining in original. Joseph Smith had announced this name earlier to the Council of Fifty, and the name referred not only to the commonwealth to be established but to the council itself, which was conceptualized as the commonwealth in embryo. See Andrew F. Ehat, "'It Seems Like Heaven Began on Earth': Joseph Smith and the Constitution of the Kingdom of God," *Brigham Young University Studies* 20, no. 3 (1980): 253–79.

21. Council of Fifty, Minutes, April 18, 1844, in *JSP*, CFM:112.

22. See US Constitution, art. 6, cl. 2.

23. Council of Fifty, Minutes, April 18, 1844, in *JSP*, CFM:110.

24. While it has been argued that the political theory behind section 134 comes out of the political theory of the Scottish Enlightenment as filtered through the founding generation, Fred Gedicks has persuasively argued that its account of political sovereignty differs markedly from the standard account of American constitutional law. Compare Rodney K. Smith, "James Madison,

John Witherspoon, and Oliver Cowdery: The First Amendment and the 134th Section of the Doctrine and Covenants," *Brigham Young University Law Review* 2003, no. 3 Spring (2003): 891–940; Frederick Mark Gedicks, "The Embarrassing Section 134," *Brigham Young University Law Review* 2003, no. Spring (2003): 959–72.

25. Council of Fifty, Minutes, April 18, 1844, in *JSP*, CFM:111, underlining in original.

26. Compare Thomas Hobbes, *Leviathan: Or, The Matter, Forme, & Power of a Common-Wealth Ecclesiasticall and Civill* (New York: Barnes & Noble Books, 2004), 77. Indeed, in its uncompromising insistence on the exclusive sovereignty of God, the preamble bears more resemblance to classical Islamic legal theories than to the liberal and republican traditions from which the US Constitution emerged. As one historian of Islamic law summed up the classical theory, "Law is the command of God; and the acknowledged function of Muslim jurisprudence, from the beginning, was simply the discovery of the terms of that command." Noel J. Coulson, *A History of Islamic Law* (Edinburgh: Edinburgh University Press, 1964), 75. See also Nathan B. Oman, "Preaching to the Court House and Judging in the Temple," *Brigham Young University Law Review* 2009, no. 1 (2009): 185–87.

27. Council of Fifty, Minutes, April 18, 1844, in *JSP*, CFM:111–12, underlining in original.

28. Council of Fifty, Minutes, April 18, 1844, in *JSP*, CFM:113.

29. US Constitution, art 1, sec. 1.

30. Council of Fifty, Minutes, April 18, 1844, in *JSP*, CFM:113.

31. An unsigned February 1844 editorial in the *Times and Seasons* supporting Joseph Smith's bid for the US presidency stated similar themes. "Who Shall Be Our Next President," *Times and Seasons*, February 15, 1844, 439–41.

32. Council of Fifty, Minutes, April 18, 1844, in *JSP*, CFM:113–14.

33. Compare Richard Lyman Bushman, "The Theology of Councils," in *In Revelation, Reason, and Faith: Essays in Honor of Truman G. Madsen*, ed. Donald W. Parry, Daniel C. Peterson, and Stephen D. Ricks (Provo, UT: FARMS, 2002), 433–46.

34. Council of Fifty, Minutes, April 18, 1844, in *JSP*, CFM:114.

35. Council of Fifty, Minutes, September 9, 1845, in *JSP*, CFM:467.

36. The process here illustrates how some revealed texts within Mormonism were produced. While the constitution has the Lord speaking in the first person, the

document itself was the product of a committee and contains clear instances of borrowing from other texts. The committee seem to have understood the voice of the Lord to have been less a matter of taking down divine dictation than of producing a text that they felt confident expressed divine intentions. Compare Scott H. Faulring, "An Examination of the 1829 'Articles of the Church of Christ' in Relation to Section 20 of the Doctrine and Covenants," *Brigham Young University Studies* 43, no. 4 (Winter 2004): 57–91.

37. Council of Fifty, Minutes, April 25, 1844, in *JSP*, CFM:135.

38. Council of Fifty, Minutes, April 25, 1844, in *JSP*, CFM:135–37. While the written constitution produced by Taylor, Richards, Phelps, and Pratt lodged virtually all power in a single "Prophet whom I have called and chosen," Joseph Smith's revelation addresses a plural audience who are collectively made the constitution. This is consistent with the tendency that Richard Bushman has noted of Joseph Smith to disperse prophetic authority into councils. See Bushman, "Theology of Councils."

39. See Kathleen Flake, *The Politics of American Religious Identity: The Seating of Senator Reed Smoot, Mormon Apostle* (Chapel Hill: University of North Carolina Press, 2004).

40. "Cannon on Politics," *Salt Lake Herald*, September 16, 1897, 5. There is no contemporary evidence that Joseph Smith participated in the effort to draft the written constitution for the kingdom of God. Cannon was not a member of the Council of Fifty at the time, although he was later close to men who were. Strikingly, Cannon's remarks allude to the recent decision to drop Moses Thatcher from the Quorum of the Twelve as a result of conflicts with the First Presidency over the role of church leaders in partisan politics. The controversy was one of the first steps towards defining the more limited political role of the Church in the post-Manifesto era. See Kenneth W. Godfrey, "Moses Thatcher in the Dock: His Trials, the Aftermath, and His Last Days," *Journal of Mormon History* 24, no. 1 (1998): 54–88; Edward Leo Lyman, "The Alienation of an Apostle from His Quorum: The Moses Thatcher Case," *Dialogue: A Journal of Mormon Thought* 18 (Spring 1985): 67–91.

41. Patrick Q. Mason, "God and the People: Theodemocracy in Nineteenth-Century Mormonism," *Journal of Church and State* 55, no. 3 (Summer 2013): 373–75.

42. See, for example, Benjamin F. Johnson's comments in his autobiography, quoted in Jedediah S. Rogers, ed., *The Council of Fifty: A Documentary History* (Salt Lake City: Signature Books, 2014), 32.

43. Kathleen Flake has documented a similar dynamic in this period, during which Joseph Smith's accounts of the First Vision first gained wide prominence and the early efforts to preserve Mormon historic sites were made, allowing Joseph F. Smith and other turn-of-the-century Mormons to claim the history of the Restoration, even as they abandoned polygamy and dramatically transformed the meaning of Latter-day Saint Zion building. See Flake, *Politics of American Religious Identity*, 109–37.

Chapter 7

LOST TEACHINGS OF JOSEPH SMITH, BRIGHAM YOUNG, AND OTHER CHURCH LEADERS

Gerrit J. Dirkmaat

The publication of the record of the Nauvoo Council of Fifty by *The Joseph Smith Papers* (*JSP*) and the Church History Department of the Church of Jesus Christ of Latter-day Saints is easily one of the most important events of the last decade for expanding our understanding of early Mormon history. Only the *JSP*'s publication of the Book of Commandments and Revelations, the earliest record of many of Joseph Smith's revelations, rivals the publication of this important document, which has hitherto been inaccessible to historians. For those who have hungered after the new material that is being brought to light by the *JSP*, the Council of Fifty record not only contains precious nuggets but is a veritable treasure trove of new information. Researchers will learn much about the last few months of Joseph Smith's life and the dramatic, event-filled months that followed, culminating in the Mormons' winter departure from Nauvoo.

For members of the Church who may see examining such a massive record as a daunting prospect, they may be most interested in the teachings and insights of Joseph Smith, Brigham Young, and other Church leaders contained in the record. Because the record of the Council of Fifty has never been published before, many of these apostolic and prophetic teachings have been lost to history until now. Some of these priceless insights will no doubt eventually make their way into lesson manuals, general conference talks, Sunday School lessons, and other Latter-day Saint literature. This article will highlight many of these teachings.

JOSEPH SMITH ON THE FUNCTION AND PURPOSE OF COUNCILS

The Council of Fifty was organized with men from many different backgrounds. Some had been members of the Church from the earliest years; some had converted only recently. Some hailed from southern states, some northern, and others came from Canada or England. In fact, three members of the council were not members of the church at all, a point Joseph Smith wanted recorded and heralded. Joseph Smith taught how such an eclectic group could have productive meetings.

Council clerk William Clayton recorded in one of the earliest meetings, "Presᵗ Joseph said he wanted all the brethren to speak their minds on this subject and to say what was in their hearts whether good or bad. He did not want to be forever surrounded by a set of 'dough heads' and if they did not rise up and shake themselves and exercise themselves in discussing these important matters he should consider them nothing better than 'dough heads.'"[1]

A few weeks later Joseph provided further instructions on the importance of sharing differing thoughts and opinions in councils. Clayton recorded that Joseph "commenced by showing, that the reason why men always failed to establish important measures was, because in their organization they never could agree to disagree long enough to select the pure gold from the dross by the process of investigation."[2]

The council made various assignments to committees and individuals. The members of one committee, charged with the daunting task of writing a constitution for the kingdom of God (that is, the council), were unsure how to proceed. Feeling the weight of such an assignment, worried that what they produced would not be acceptable to the Lord or to other members of the council, they asked if Joseph Smith would join with them to aid them in crafting their document. In response, Joseph explained the necessity of his remaining separate from such discussions. He wanted the committee members to struggle to find all the truth they could and then bring the document to him for inspired correction. Perhaps Joseph realized that if he

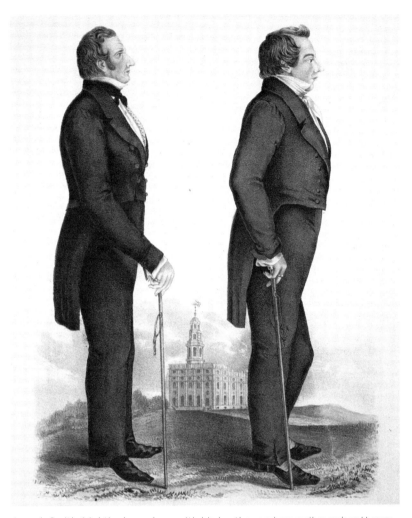

Joseph Smith (right), shown here with his brother and council member Hyrum Smith (left), encouraged council members to candidly share their views. Attributed to Sutcliffe Maudsley. Courtesy of Church History Museum.

were part of the committee, the members would be too deferential to him and would not learn to search for truth and to make up their own minds. He also wanted the men to see the limits of their own wisdom.

> Prest J. Smith arose and said that the committee were first appointed to bring forth all the intelligence they could, and when their

productions were presented to him he could correct the errors and fill the interstices where it was lacking. He had considered that a Theocracy consisted in our exercising all the intelligence of the council, and bringing forth all the light which dwells in the breast of every man, and then let God approve of the document & receiveing the sanction of the council it becomes a law. Theocracy as he understands it is, for the people to get the voice of God and then acknowledge it, and see it executed. It is necessary for the council to exhaust their wisdom, and except they do they will never know but they are as wise as God himself and ambitious men will, like Lucifer think they are as wise as God and will try to lift themselves up and put their foot on the necks of others. There has always been some man to put himself forward and say I am the great I &c. I want the council to exert all their wisdom in this thing, and when they see that they cannot get a perfect law themselves, and I can, then, they will see from whence wisdom flows. I know I can get the voice of God on the subject. Vox populi, Vox Dei. The voice of the people assenting to the voice of God. . . . I dont want to be ranked with that committee I am a committee of myself, and cannot mingle with any committee in such matters. The station which I hold is an independant one and ought not to be mingled with any thing else. Let the Committee get all the droppings they can from the presence of God and bring it to me, and if it needs correction or enlargement I am ready to give it. The principles by which the world can be governed is the principle of two or three being united. Faith cannot exist without a concentration of two or three. The sun, moon and planets roll on that principle. If God the Father, the Son and the Holy Ghost were to disagree, the worlds would clash together in an instant. . . . From henceforth let it be understood that I shall not associate with any committee I want every man to get knowledge, search the laws of nations and get all the information they can. There can be no exceptions taken to any thing that any man can say in this council. I dont want any man ever to assent to any thing in this council and then find fault with it. Dont decide in favor of any thing untill you know it. Every man ought to study Geography, Governments and languages, so that he may be able to go forth to any nation and before any multitude with eloquence.[3]

JOSEPH SMITH ON RELIGIOUS TOLERANCE AND DEFENDING RELIGIOUS FREEDOM

During the April 11, 1844, meeting of the council, Joseph gave a moving sermon on the importance of religious liberty. Having been on the receiving end of local, state, and federal government failures to protect Mormons and their rights, Joseph insisted that any government formed by God and every member of the council should respect and protect the rights of every religious group. Poignantly, and perhaps with a notion that his own death was approaching, Joseph extolled the virtues of friendship and ominously confided, "The only thing I am afraid of is, that I will not live long enough to enjoy the society of these my friends as long as I want to."[4] William Clayton not only captured the words spoken by Joseph in detail but also attempted to convey the passion with which Joseph spoke, concluding the account by explaining, "While the president was speaking on these subjects he felt animated and used a 24 inch gauge or rule pretty freely till finally he broke it in two in the middle."[5]

> For the benifit of mankind and succeeding generations he [Joseph Smith] wished it to be recorded that there are men admitted members of this honorable council, who are not members of the church of Jesus Christ of Latter Day Saints, neither profess any creed or religious sentiment whatever, to show that in the organization of this kingdom men are not consulted as to their religious opinions or notions in any shape or form whatever and that we act upon the broad and liberal principal that all men have equal rights, and ought to be respected, and that every man has a privilege in this organization of choosing for himself voluntarily his God, and what he pleases for his religion, inasmuch as there is no danger but that every man will embrace the greatest light. God cannot save or damn a man only on the principle that every man acts, chooses and worships for himself; hence the importance of thrusting from us every spirit of bigotry and intolerance towards a mans religious sentiments, that spirit which has drenched the earth with blood— When a man feels the least temptation to such intollerance he ought to spurn it from him. It becomes our duty on account of this intollerance and corruption—the inalienable right of

man being to think as he pleases—worship as he pleases &c being the first law of every thing that is sacred—to guard every ground all the days of our lives. I will appeal to every man in this council beginning at the youngest that when he arrives to the years of Hoary age he will have to say that the principles of intollerance and bigotry never had a place in this kingdom, nor in my breast, and that he is even then ready to die rather than yeild to such things. Nothing can reclaim the human mind from its ignorance, bigotry, superstition &c but those grand and sublime principles of equal rights and universal freedom to all men. We must not despise a man on account of infirmity. We ought to love a man more for his infirmity. Nothing is more congenial to my feelings and principles, than the principles of universal freedom and has been from the beginning. If I can know that a man is susceptible of good feelings & integrity and will stand by his friends, he is my friend. The only thing I am afraid of is, that I will not live long enough to enjoy the society of these my friends as long as I want to. Let us from henceforth drive from us every species of intollerance. When a man is free from it he is capable of being a critic. When I have used every means in my power to exalt a mans mind, and have taught him righteous principles to no effect—he is still inclined in his darkness, yet the same principles of liberty and charity would ever be manifested by me as though he embraced it. Hence in all governments or political transactions a mans religious opinions should never be called in question. A man should be judged by the law independant of religious prejudice, hence we want in our constitution those laws which would require all its officers to administer justice without any regard to his religious opinions, or thrust him from his office. There is only two or three things lacking in the constitution of the United States. If they had said all men born equal, and not only that but they shall have their rights, they shall be free, or the armies of the government should be compelled to enforce those principles of liberty. And the President or Governor who does not do this, and who does not enforce those principles he shall lose his head. When a man is thus bound by a constitution he cannot refuse to protect his subjects, he dare not do it. And when a Governor or president will not protect his subjects he ought to be put away from his office.

. . . When a man can enjoy his liberties and has the power of civil officers to protect him, how happy he is.[6]

BRIGHAM YOUNG AND JOHN TAYLOR ON CONTINUING REVELATION

In their efforts to discern how best to create a new constitution for the coming kingdom of God on earth, council members shared multiple viewpoints. Some were hesitant to write a draft of the constitution for fear of making a mistake. Responding to the discussions by reminding council members of Joseph Smith's prophetic authority, senior apostle Brigham Young declared that

> he had no fears but God would organize the kingdom right, and what he has seen in this assembly was nothing more than what he had looked for. At the first meeting, when the president [Joseph Smith] stated that this was the commencement of the organization of the kingdom of God. He then felt as exalted views as he could do. He contemplated kings, governments as they are. They sunk into oblivion when he compared them with this kingdom, which was only in embryo, and it would soon send forth its influence throughout the nations. There will no doubt be a regular organization. He has heard much said on the subject of bringing forth a constitution, but he considered himself highly honored to have this privilege of being accounted a fool, that when we had done all we were capable to do, we could have the Lord speak and tell us what is right. There is a great deal allready written We can form to ourselves independant of the word of the Lord the best system of government on the earth; but after all this, when we have done all the Lord will make it just right. He can form a constitution by which he is willing to be governed. He is willing to be ruled by the means which God will appoint. He dont believe we can adopt laws for the government of people in futurity. We can, for the time being, point out laws for present necessities. He supposed there has not yet been a perfect revelation given, because we cannot understand it, yet we receive a little here and a little there. He should not be stumbled if the prophet should translate the bible forty thousand

times over and yet it should be different in some places every time, because when God speake, he always speaks according to the capacity of the people. The starting point for the government of the kingdom is in the Book of Doctrine and Covenants, but he does not know how much more there is in the bosom of the Almighty. When God sees that his people have enlarged upon what he has given us he will give us more. The sta[r]ting point is here, but God has not come here, He has sent his agent, his minister to act in his name. And if he has got an agent to dictate to us here the organization is here. When a man is clothed with authority to do all business for those who sent him, what he does [is?] right, and this is the kind of agent we have got, and God appointed him We did not appoint him. If the Lord Almighty calls upon one of his servants as a minister, the nation to whom he is sent has no control over him whatever. If the Latter Day Saints believe that our prophet is fallen what are they going to do? How will they help themselves? It is the prerogative of the Almighty to differ from his subjects in what he pleases, or how, or when he pleases, and what will they do; they must bow to it, or kick themselves to death, or to hell. He [Joseph Smith] can disagree with the whole church as he has a mind, and how? Because he is a perfect committee of himself. . . . He would rather have the pure revelations of Jesus Christ as they now stand, to carry to the nations, than any thing else.[7]

In this same meeting, apostle John Taylor shared similar sentiments about revelation flowing from God through his prophet. As a member of the committee assigned to draft the new constitution, Taylor poignantly felt the need for revelation through Joseph Smith:

If they can get intelligence from God they can write correct principles, if not, they cannot. He was always convinced that no power can guide us right but the wisdom of God. It needed a revelation from God to shew the very first principles of the kingdom of God. No one knew how to baptize or lay on hands untill it was revealed through our chairman. National affairs are equally as far fallen and degenerate as religious matters. This nation is as far fallen and degenerate as any nation under heaven. When we were in the world, we were ignorant with regard to correct principles. We are now a little differently situated. We have a portion of the spirit, but if we get the document any where right it will be because God gives it; and if not, we know nothing but what either you [Joseph Smith] or God teaches us.[8]

HYRUM SMITH ON THE FULFILLMENT OF PROPHECY AND THE EXERCISE OF FAITH

The council record also contains a few brief statements of Hyrum Smith. One of the founding members of the council and the patriarch of the Church, Hyrum spoke rarely in this venue, but each time he did, he spoke wholeheartedly in support of his brother Joseph and the aim of establishing the kingdom of God on earth:

> Hyrum Smith followed the chairman and said that the time was at hand when the prophecies should be fulfilled, when the nations were ready to embrace the gospel and when the ensign should be lift up and the standard to the people and he believed if we will set up the standard and raise the ensign the honest in heart of all nations will immediately begin to flock to the standard of our God.[9]

On another occasion, Hyrum stated that the

> observations by our Pres[t.] so well accorded with his own feelings that he wanted to say a few words. When Moses was appointed to lead the people, God gave him Aaron to speak for him. When God called Enoch he wanted to know why God had done so inasmuch as he was an illiterate man

The council records contain teachings of Hyrum Smith and other Church leaders. Photograph of painting by "Webber," circa 1833. Courtesy of Church History Library, Salt Lake City.

&c. God told him to go forth and he would justify his words. Enoch went forth in the exercise of faith, not in the exercise of great words. God walked with him 300 years. Moses had power. before him Mount Sinai trembled and shook to the centre. Had Moses not gone forth in the exercise of faith he would not have accomplished the work which God sent him to do. We stand in the same light. We have greater power and are called to do a greater work. We have more power than Enoch and have a greater work to do than Enoch had and we shall accomplish it." He then referred to the principles of a Theocracy and hopes every man will get into the spirit of his calling.[10]

JOSEPH SMITH ON THE KINGDOM OF GOD VERSUS THE CHURCH OF GOD

One of the primary purposes of the Council of Fifty was to seek to establish the physical, or political, kingdom of God on earth. It planned for a government organization that would allow the Saints to worship God freely and construct a government on theocratic principles in whatever land they eventually settled upon. Naturally, this purpose of the council led to questions on the difference between the kingdom and the Church. Since so many Church leaders were at the head of the movement to create this new government, what would be the difference between the two entities? Joseph Smith provided that answer as well as commentary on the deficiency of the US Constitution in one key area:

> There is a distinction between the Church of God and kingdom of God. The laws of the kingdom are not designed to effect our salvation hereafter. It is an entire, distinct and separate government. The church is a spiritual matter and a spiritual kingdom; but the kingdom which Daniel saw was not a spiritual kingdom, but was designed to be got up for the safety and salvation of the saints by protecting them in their religious rights and worship. Any thing that would tolerate man in the worship of his God under his own vine and fig-tree would be tolerated of God. The literal kingdom of God, and the church of God are two distinct things. The gifts of prophets, evangelists &c never were designed to govern men in civil matters. The kingdom of

God has nothing to do with giving commandments to damn a man spiritually. It only has power to make a man amenable to his fellow man. God gave commandments that if a man killed &c he should be killed himself, but it did not damn him. In relation to the constitution of the United States, there is but one difficulty, and that is, the constitution provides the things which we want but lacks the power to carry the laws into effect. We want to alter it so as to make it imperative on the officers to enforce the protection of all men in their rights

He then shewed how the constitution ought to be amended.

Men are complaining all over the United States, and we have the most reason to complain.[11]

JOSEPH SMITH RECEIVES A REVELATION FOR THE COUNCIL

After many discussions about what language should be included in the proposed constitution for the kingdom of God on earth, Joseph Smith received a revelation to put the matter to rest. The revelation was never canonized but was reported in the later Utah-era council minutes.[12] The original minutes of the meeting capture the receipt of this unpublished revelation:

The chairman then made some further remarks and advised that we let the constitution alone.

He would tell us the whole matter about the constitution as follows—

Verily thus saith the Lord, ye are my constitution, and I am your God, and ye are my spokesmen. From henceforth do as I shall command you. Saith the Lord.[13]

JOSEPH SMITH ON NOT JUDGING OTHERS AND ON AVOIDING SINFUL ACTS

In the council meeting held on May 3, 1844, there was apparently some objection to one of the newly proposed members of the council because of past transgressions. Joseph Smith taught:

We have no right to complain of others while we are as corrupt as they are. . . .

We should never indulge our appetites to injure our influence, or wound the feelings of friends, or cause the spirit of the Lord to leave us. There is no excuse for any man to drink and get drunk in the church of Christ, or gratify any appetite, or lust, contrary to the principles of righteousness.

The chairman continued to instruct the council on the principles of sobriety, and every thing pertaining to godliness at considerable length & concluded by remarking that it is best to run on a long race and be careful to keep good wind &c.[14]

PORTER ROCKWELL'S BITTER REACTION TO JOSEPH SMITH'S MURDER

When council meetings resumed in 1845 after the murder of Joseph Smith, several council members, including Porter Rockwell, expressed raw emotions at the loss. Because few of Rockwell's contemporary statements exist, these words give rare insight into his passionate character and love for Joseph Smith.

O. P. Rockwell said I say yes to every thing that is good and right. . . . I was a friend to Joseph Smith while he lived. I am still his friend. He cant avenge his wrongs himself, but I mean to avenge them for him, and if I get into trouble I want you to help me if you can without criminating yourselves if not, let me go. I love my friends and hate my enemies. I cant love them if I would.[15]

JOHN TAYLOR ON MISTREATMENT OF THE MORMONS

In the aftermath of Joseph Smith's murder and the continued threats of violence against Mormons in Illinois, several men in the council expressed their indignation both toward their persecutors and toward the government that refused to help the Mormons remain in Nauvoo in peace. John Taylor, still recovering from wounds received at Carthage, had lost all

John Taylor, injured in the attacks that killed Joseph and Hyrum Smith, expressed exasperation and outrage toward government officials. Photograph, circa 1852, likely by Marsena Cannon. Courtesy of Church History Library, Salt Lake City.

faith in the willingness of the American democracy to defend the rights of a despised minority. His exasperation, bitterness, and anger are demonstrated in these remarks from March 1845:

> In regard to the situation of the world as it now exists I dont care a damn because they are as corrupt as the devil. We have no benifit from the laws of the land, and the only reason why they dont cut our throats is because they dare not, and as brother [Heber C.] Kimball

says I dont care how often the bucket is turned up. Some cry out it will bring persecution, but they cannot lie about us, nor persecute us worse than they have done, and I go in for whipping the scoundrels when they come into our midst and if any of them come near me I will use my cane to them and I want my brethren to go and do likewise. This cursed Bettisworth [David Bettisworth, a constable] was here prowling round the City a few days ago. He was one who was trying to push our brethren into the Jail at Carthage, and he wanted to have them taken out without a guard that they might be shot down by the mob before they got to the Jail. I dont want such men to come near us, and if they come near me I feel like whipping them I dont care about excitement, we can stand it as long as they can. We know we have no more justice here, no more than we could get at the gates of hell, and the only thing we have got to do is to take care of ourselves. As to the other thing which has been proposed about seeking out a location in the West I don't care how soon it go into operation. People talk about law and justice I go in for giving them the same kind of justice they give us. . . . I go in for a company being sent out to find out place where we can establish the kingdom, erect the standard and dwell in peace, and have our own laws.[16]

BRIGHAM YOUNG ON SETTLING IN THE GREAT SALT LAKE AREA

Many of the later council meetings in Nauvoo are filled with discussions about precisely when the Mormons should leave Nauvoo and where they should go. Brigham Young felt he was carrying out Joseph Smith's intention to settle in the mountains of the West. Some raised concerns that the Rocky Mountains were too high, too isolated, or too cold. Young responded that those misgivings were precisely why he wanted to settle there: to protect the Mormons from potential conflicts with other settlers as had happened in Ohio, Missouri, and Illinois. Instead, Young wanted a place where "we can gather by thousands and dwell in peace."[17]

Young sought a place where the Mormons could live and practice their religion without interference or harassment from mobs and the local, state, and national governments that had proven themselves at best indifferent and ineffectual in their responses to violence perpetrated against Mormons. At worst, those vaunted democratic institutions had at times conspired with the militant antagonists that sought to drive the Mormons first from Missouri and then from Illinois. Young and other members of the council believed they needed to find a place free from the tyranny that often resulted from unrestrained American democracy. At the March 1, 1845, council meeting, Young declared:

> The propriety of fitting out this company for this expedition is what we want to enter into, how many shall go, and who, or whether any. We know this was one of Josephs measures and my feelings are, if we cannot have the priviledge of carrying out Josephs measures I would rather lie down and have my head cut off at once. To carry out Josephs measures is sweeter to me than the honey or the honey comb. I want to see the Lamanites come in by thousands and the time has come. While Joseph was living it seems as though he was hurried by the Lord all the time, and especially for the last year. It seemed he laid out work for this church which would last them twenty years to carry out. I used to wonder why it was, that he used to be hurried so, not supposing he was going to die, but now I understand the reason. With regard to the propriety of going ahead in this thing we are all of one mind. With regard to how and when and where to begin is what we what we want to investigate. I have no doubt or dubiety on my mind with regard to the Lord's communicating the knowlege no more than I have that I can walk home When the Twelve have been separated from Joseph in England or the Eastern States or elswhere, I defy any man to point out the time when I was in the dark in regard to what should be done. I have not been in the dark pertaining to any matter. Some have been fearful that I would blunder in the dark but it is not so. When any person has any doubt and manifest to me a fear that the Twelve or authorities of the church will blunder in the dark, it always seems nonsense to me. I know as God lives that there is no man who will always go in the way of his duty, but God will keep him right, & preserve him untill he has accomplished his work, and there would not a gun

have gone off in Carthage had not God seen that Joseph had done enough and he took him to rest.

There is no place but what we shall go along just right if we will be of one heart and one mind. The time has come when we must seek out a location. The yoke of the gentiles is broke, their doom is sealed, there is not the least fibre can possibly be discovered that binds us to the gentile world. It is for us to take care of ourselves and go and pick out a place where we can go and dwell in peace after we have finished the houses and got our endowment, not but that the Lord can give it to us in the wilderness, but I have no doubt we shall get it here. But we want a home where we can gather by thousands and dwell in peace. . . .

These are some matters laying before us and I want the brethren to speak their minds freely. I want the brethren to be patient stop and consider and dont get in a hurry. We can stop as long as we like, and meet as often as we have a mind to. Don't be in a hurry. We are in eternity and have all eternity before us, and there is no need to be in a hurry.[18]

Later that year, Young identified the area of the Great Salt Lake as the intended destination:

The chairman [Young] then stated that it is well understood by this council the views of Joseph in regard to setting up the kingdom in some place where we can exalt the standard and enjoy liberty. We have sent some men this spring and have learned considerable of the feelings of the Indians towards us, and the prospect is good. The Temple is near finished and many of the brethren will no doubt receive their endowment this winter. We have contemplated sending a company west next spring, and this is what we want to take into consideration. It has been proved that there is not much difficulty in sending people beyond the mountains. We have designed sending them somewhere near the Great Salt Lake.[19]

After Illinois governor Thomas Ford deliberately falsified reports of a federal army marching on Nauvoo and as other rumors began circulating of impending conflict, Young and the council made immediate plans to depart even though it was the middle of winter. Responding to the concerns about the climate and the isolation of the proposed Great Basin settlement, Young explained in a January 1846 meeting:

> Now if we go between the mountains to the place under consideration there will be no jealousies from any nation, but if we stop this side the mountains there will be complaints which will reach us. There have been some objections to the country because the land is high, but it is surrounded by very high mountains which would moderate the climate very much. If we can get to this place we can strengthen ourselves and be better able to grapple with our foes. . . . If we should [go?] there we can sustain ourselves comfortably and it will soon become the greatest market in America for all kinds of the productions of the soil. At the same time, we would fill up all the country to the coast and soon hold the balance of power over the whole country. Then, if they will give us a portion of the country we will defend their flag for the time being, and if they did not walk up to their agreement we could make them and set up our own standard. Ten thousand men would do more to sustain us there, than two hundred thousand would on the coast. After we get there the first thing he would do, would be to fortify ourselves, which could easily be done, and he should almost feel like fortifying before he took time to pray. If it is a cold country, and a hard country to live in we wont be envied, but if we go to a good country before we are able to defend it we would be troubled with mobs as we are here.[20]

CONCLUSION

These selected sermons, teachings, and discussions found in the Nauvoo Council of Fifty record not only demonstrate the value of this new publication but also typify the insights that can be gained about the various individuals whose discussions were recorded in this minute book. Readers will get to view many of the most prominent leaders of the Church in the late Nauvoo period as they grappled with ongoing threats of violence, religious questions, the logistics of a cross-continental emigration, apostasy, and the murder of Joseph Smith and his brother Hyrum. Few sources paint this kind of candid, multifaceted portrait of the personalities that members of the Church have come to revere as prophets and apostles.

NOTES

1. Council of Fifty, Minutes, March 10, 1844, in Matthew J. Grow, Ronald K. Esplin, Mark Ashurst-McGee, Gerrit J. Dirkmaat, and Jeffrey D. Mahas, eds., *Council of Fifty, Minutes, March 1844–January 1846*, vol. 1 of the Administrative Records series of *The Joseph Smith Papers*, ed. Ronald K. Esplin, Matthew J. Grow, and Matthew C. Godfrey (Salt Lake City: Church Historian's Press, 2016), 39 (hereafter *JSP*, CFM).

2. Council of Fifty, Minutes, April 4, 1844, in *JSP*, CFM: 79.

3. Council of Fifty, Minutes, April 11, 1844, in *JSP*, CFM:91–93.

4. Council of Fifty, Minutes, April 11, 1844, in *JSP*, CFM:100.

5. Council of Fifty, Minutes, April 11, 1844, in *JSP*, CFM:101.

6. Council of Fifty, Minutes, April 11, 1844, in *JSP*, CFM:97–101.

7. Council of Fifty, Minutes, April 18, 1844, in *JSP*, CFM:119–20.

8. Council of Fifty, Minutes, April 18, 1844, in *JSP*, CFM:114–15.

9. Council of Fifty, Minutes, March 19, 1844, in *JSP*, CFM:52.

10. Council of Fifty, Minutes, April 11, 1844, in *JSP*, CFM:93–94.

11. Council of Fifty, Minutes, April 18, 1844, in *JSP*, CFM:128–29.

12. Council of Fifty, Minutes, April 10, 1880, in L. John Nuttall, Notebook, 1880–82, Council of Fifty, Papers, 1845–83, Church History Library, Salt Lake City; see also Franklin D. Richards, Journals, 1844–1899, entry for April 10, 1880, Church History Library.

13. Council of Fifty, Minutes, April 25, 1844, in *JSP*, CFM:135–37.

14. Council of Fifty, Minutes, May 3, 1844, in *JSP*, CFM:139–40.

15. Council of Fifty, Minutes, February 4, 1845, in *JSP*, CFM:223–24.

16. Council of Fifty, Minutes, March 1, 1845, in *JSP*, CFM:264–65.

17. Council of Fifty, Minutes, March 1, 1845, in *JSP*, CFM:258.

18. Council of Fifty, Minutes, March 1, 1845, in *JSP*, CFM:257–58, 260.

19. Council of Fifty, Minutes, September 9, 1845, in *JSP*, CFM:471–72.

20. Council of Fifty, Minutes, January 11, 1846, in *JSP*, CFM:518–19.

Chapter 8

INSIGHTS INTO MORMON RECORD-KEEPING PRACTICES FROM THE COUNCIL OF FIFTY MINUTES

R. Eric Smith

I have been an editor and manager with the Joseph Smith Papers Project for more than a decade. The project's publications fall into the well-established genre of documentary editing, meaning the focus is on presenting the texts of the original documents with the historical information needed to understand the circumstances of their creation. One of the major contributions of the project's historians and archivists has been to shed light on the world of early Mormon record keeping, particularly with respect to the papers of Joseph Smith. Who inscribed and revised these documents, when, and in what capacity? For what purposes were the documents created? How do the documents relate to one another? How were the documents transmitted, used, filed, and preserved? How reliable are the documents? For documentary editors, the answers to these and similar questions can be as important as the content of the documents themselves.

As the other essays in this collection help demonstrate, the content of the recently published record of the Nauvoo Council of Fifty is invaluable in helping historians and others understand Mormon history from the late Nauvoo period to the exodus west and beyond. Council clerk William Clayton's record is also fascinating when interrogated *as* a record—that is, through questions such as those listed above. My essay shares a few insights into and questions about Clayton's record from the standpoint of a documentary editor.

CONFIDENTIALITY OF THE MINUTES

The life story of the minutes, from their initial creation by Clayton down to the present, is interesting in its own right, and I provide a brief summary here for that reason and to help introduce my other observations about them. A key element of the story is confidentiality. The members of the council took a confidentiality oath upon joining the council, and many council discussions reemphasized the importance of secrecy. Clayton evidently began keeping minutes on loose paper at the preliminary council meeting on March 10, 1844,[1] but the minutes of the initial March meetings were burned after the March 14 meeting out of fear they could be used against the members of the council. Nevertheless, Clayton continued keeping minutes after March 14. A few days before his death, Joseph Smith ordered Clayton to send away, burn, or bury the council records. Clayton buried them in his garden and dug them up a few days later—another Mormon record coming out of the ground.

It was apparently after this that Clayton began reconstructing the destroyed minutes and copying surviving loose minutes in the three bound volumes (sometimes referred to as the "fair copy," meaning a neat and final copy) that survive today. When the council was revived in early 1845 under Brigham Young, a pattern was established of the loose minutes being read at the subsequent meeting and then burned. Clayton kept a permanent copy of the minutes in the bound volumes, but it is not clear if other members of the council even knew of the fair copy. After the exodus to Utah, the records and proceedings of the council continued to be closely guarded. For example, in December 1880, council recorder George Q. Cannon referred to the Council of "Kanalima" when he wrote about the council in a letter to Joseph F. Smith ("kanalima" is the Hawaiian word for "fifty"; both Cannon and Smith had been missionaries to Hawaii in their youth). Eventually, Clayton's record became part of the First Presidency's collection, where it remained closed to access until the twenty-first century.[2]

That the record was closed was obviously a challenge for the Joseph Smith Papers Project, which intended to publish a comprehensive edition of Joseph Smith documents and had repeatedly advertised that fact. The question of whether the project would publish these records was seen by some observers as a sort of acid test of the project's credibility—if the project could not publish the Council of Fifty minutes, it could not claim to be transparent (much less comprehensive). Project scholars remained hopeful that permission to access and publish the Joseph Smith–era Council of Fifty records would be given. While for years we waited and hoped permission would come, we focused on producing an edition that both would satisfy high scholarly standards and would serve the Church's interests in fostering reputable scholarship on the Church's history. We also paused work for a period of time on the third volume of Joseph Smith's journals, covering May 1843 through June 1844, because we wanted the annotation in that volume to be informed by the Council of Fifty minutes.[3] Eventually, in 2010, project scholars were given access to the records and permission to publish them.

The council minutes are one of several records from the First Presidency's collection that have been made available to the project for either publication or research in the last dozen years. Other examples include Revelation Book 1 (or the "Book of Commandments and Revelations"), Joseph Smith's first Nauvoo journal (contained in the record book titled "The Book of the Law of the Lord"), and three drafts of the early portion of Joseph Smith's manuscript history project.[4]

It should be noted that the council minutes are not the only Joseph Smith record containing material that Joseph and his associates viewed as confidential. The early editions of the Doctrine and Covenants, for example, used code words in some revelations to conceal the identities of Church leaders involved with Church businesses.[5] In Joseph Smith's Nauvoo journals, his scribe Willard Richards used shorthand to record especially sensitive information, such as information about plural marriages.[6] Richards also attempted to conceal certain aspects of council-related discussions in the journal by writing some words backward. In the March 10, 1844, entry, in which he summarized the initial meeting of the council, Richards wrote Texas as "Saxet," Pinery as "Yrenip," Santa Fe as "Atnas Eef," and Houston as "Notsuoh."[7] This code is about the simplest one imaginable, useful probably only to throw off someone who would take a quick glance at the journal.

To me, the recording and preservation of confidential information shows how serious Church clerks were about keeping records. Why else the paradox of writing down something that you want kept hid? Why not just avoid recording in the first place?

IMPORTANCE OF KEEPING A RECORD

At the close of Clayton's minutes for the council meeting on March 14, 1844, we find this surprising passage: "It was considered wisdom to burn the minutes in consequence of treachery and plots of designing men."[8] Given that the council's plans to improve upon the US Constitution and to explore settlements outside the nation's boundaries could be seen as controversial, if not treasonous (and publicizing such plans could have led to interference with them), it makes sense that council members would want to keep their business confidential. Why then did Clayton keep minutes of those initial meetings in the first place? And—a more arresting question—after burning the earliest minutes, why did Clayton *continue* minute taking and then later reconstruct the discussions of those earliest meetings, even when Church leaders worried so much about keeping their discussions confidential?

The answer must be that Church leaders, or at least Clayton, had become thoroughly convinced of the importance or even vitality of record keeping— perhaps so much so that keeping records had moved to the level of habit. Of course, record keeping had been emphasized both explicitly and implicitly in the Church's scripture. In the Book of Mormon, for example, Enos prays that the Nephite records will be preserved, and the resurrected Christ himself inspects the Nephite records and finds them deficient. In the revelation given the day the Church was organized, God commanded the Church to keep a record.[9] The fullest explication on the importance and purposes of record keeping had come from Joseph Smith in instructions he gave the Quorum of the Twelve Apostles shortly after the quorum was organized in February 1835. The oft-quoted passage is too long to be repeated here, but in it Joseph Smith gave a number of reasons that records should be kept: they would serve as precedent to help decide "almost any point that might be agitated"; they would help leaders more powerfully bear witness of the "great and glorious manifestations" that had been made known to them; leaders would later find passages of these records personally inspiring—"a feast" to their "own souls"; God would be angry and the Spirit would withdraw if leaders did not sufficiently value and preserve what God had given them; and if leaders were falsely accused of crimes, records would help prove that they were "somewhere else" at the time.[10]

While we can only guess as to whether particular members of the council had any of these objectives in mind with respect to the record Clayton was keeping (indeed, it is not clear that the members realized Clayton was copying his loose minutes into a bound record[11]), we get one more glimpse into Joseph's views on the importance of records a few days before his murder. At about one o'clock in the morning on June 23, 1844, Joseph Smith, fearing for his safety in the crisis that erupted after the destruction of the *Nauvoo Expositor,* called for Clayton and gave him instructions. In his journal Clayton recorded, "Joseph whispered and told me either to put the r of k [records of the kingdom] into the hands of some faithful man and send them away, or burn them or bury them."[12] Presumably, Joseph Smith feared the records might be used against him and other Saints. Even so, he gave Clayton the option to hide the records rather than to destroy them. At this point Clayton, as one historian observed, "trusted that calmer, more reasonable and more secure times would come for the Latter-day Saints and therefore preserved the records for future generations."[13] In light of the importance that the Council of Fifty record has to understanding Mormon history, Clayton is a hero for deciding to preserve the records, even though doing so put him at personal risk.

SYSTEMATIZATION OF RECORD KEEPING

In looking at Clayton's record as a record, one of the first things we notice is that Mormon record keeping had become routinized. At the preliminary meeting of the Council of Fifty on March 10, 1844, Joseph Smith appointed William Clayton as clerk of the meeting.[14] Clayton apparently began keeping minutes that day, though, as noted above, the minutes of the earliest Council of Fifty meetings were later burned. The next day, when the council was officially organized, Joseph appointed Willard Richards as council recorder and Clayton as council clerk—Clayton was to take the minutes, and Richards perhaps had some supervisory role over Clayton. Both Richards and Clayton had significant prior experience in keeping Church records.[15]

Having two experienced clerks on the council meant that Clayton had a replacement scribe on standby if he couldn't make a meeting. This may not have been the reason that Joseph Smith appointed both a recorder and a clerk to the council, but the redundancy of roles proved handy, as Richards evidently took the complete minutes of three meetings. He was presumably also the one who took up the pen for Clayton when he had to leave one meeting partway through with a toothache.[16]

Further evidence of the routinization of Church record keeping is the high quality of Clayton's Nauvoo Council of Fifty record. His thorough, highly legible record is clearly the product of much time and care. Though Clayton presumably took original minutes on loose paper, he eventually began copying those minutes into bound volumes.[17] This process reflects awareness of broader Church record-keeping practices[18] and a consciousness to safeguard and preserve the record. As he copied the minutes, Clayton apparently used other available records, such as an attendance roll and original correspondence, to flesh them out.[19] This copying and expanding effort took considerable time and labor, as Clayton's journal indicates.[20] Even the fact that the three volumes of Clayton's record closely match one another in size and binding signals a maturing in Mormon record keeping.

We can see by comparison to earlier efforts how far the Church had come in systematizing its record-keeping practices. For example, Joseph Smith apparently did not begin copying loose manuscripts of revelations into a copy book until at least two years after he received his first revelation.[21] As another contrasting example, consider the document known by the Joseph Smith Papers as Minute Book 2, perhaps still better known as the Far West Record. This record book contains copies of minutes from Church meetings held as early as 1830 in New York, but the book as we have it was not begun until 1838 in Missouri—and was written by scribes different from those who kept the original minutes (indeed, some of the original scribes by that time had left the Church).[22] It seems probable that important information was lost as the minutes now copied into Minute Book 2 traversed this distance of time, place, and personality.

A SOLITARY EFFORT

Most of the significant Church record books from this period were created by a number of scribes working in sequence or sometimes together. For example, Joseph Smith's second letterbook, created from 1839 through the summer of 1843, was inscribed by seven different clerks. Minute Book 2, created intermittently from 1838 through 1844, was inscribed by five different clerks, who copied minutes originally kept by about twenty different clerks. The first volume of Joseph Smith's manuscript history, the only volume of that record completed before his murder, was inscribed by four clerks.[23] With these records, which were generally kept in Joseph Smith's office, the work of one scribe was likely to be seen by another. This may have created a certain accountability as to what was recorded—and an expectation that what was recorded was not completely private.

In contrast, the Nauvoo Council of Fifty record as we have it was created by one scribe, working alone and apparently in private, William Clayton. Though loose minutes of one council meeting were read at the following meeting, there is no evidence that anyone other than Clayton saw the fair copy of the minutes until the Utah period—in fact, as noted above, other council members may not have even been aware of the fair copy. It is interesting to consider how these circumstances may have affected the way Clayton created the fair copy—did this spur him on, for example, in his effort to complete the fair copy, expecting that there would never be anyone else who could complete the record for the Nauvoo period if he did not?

In this vein, I raise another question that others may wish to explore. What can we learn by considering the Nauvoo Council of Fifty record not only as an institutional record but also as a personal record of William Clayton? What can we learn of his personality or biases, his views of what initiatives or positions were wise, his individual understanding of what the council was to accomplish? If nothing else, the triumph of the detail in and the mere existence of this record shows how valuable Clayton thought the minutes of the council were and would be.

QUALITY OF RECORDS

It is always interesting to consider how various circumstances influence the quality of a particular Mormon record from this period. Joseph Smith's history notes that the deaths and faithlessness of some of his clerks, together with lawsuits, imprisonment, and poverty, had significantly interfered with the keeping of his journal and history.[24] With respect to the Council of Fifty record, it is painful to imagine how much detail from

The nearly 900-page Council of Fifty record is entirely in the handwriting of council clerk William Clayton. Photograph circa 1855. Courtesy of Church History Library, Salt Lake City.

the record was lost when the minutes of the initial meetings were burned. The March 10, 1844, preliminary meeting convened at 4:30 p.m. and met until a "late hour," with a break for dinner. And yet the minutes that Clayton reconstructed in fall 1844 are limited almost entirely to copying the two letters from the Wisconsin Saints. The pattern continues for the next few days of minutes. On March 11, the council met "all day," but the minutes take up only three pages of the record. On March 12, the council apparently met in the evening, but the record has no report, apparently because Clayton had other business that day. On March 13, the council evidently met most of the day. Clayton's report is two paragraphs. On March 14, the council met for about seven hours. Clayton: two paragraphs.[25] These meetings, held over five days straight, were the ones where two fairly innocuous letters (proposing the relocation of the Wisconsin branch to Texas) launched the formation of a new body that proposed to revise the US Constitution and that expected to "govern men in civil matters"![26] How did these men get from A to Z so quickly? The minutes here show the conclusions but so few of the reasons.

Finally, on March 19, the minutes start to become lengthier and more detailed, as now we have contemporary rather than reconstructed minutes. Even so, it is only during the period of Brigham Young's chairmanship that the minutes become consistently detailed. It is not entirely clear what changed during Young's administration, but Clayton did complain in the May 25, 1844, minutes that he could not take minutes "in full" because members were talking over one another.[27] This was after many council members had left to campaign for Joseph Smith's presidential run, and when the outside opposition that would lead to the two murders a month later was reaching a fever pitch. The editors of the minutes also postulate that the minutes from the Young era may be fuller because Clayton copied his loose minutes closer to the times of the meetings being reported, meaning he could use his memory to flesh out his raw minutes.[28]

HUMOR IN THE RECORD?

There is an example of humor in the Council of Fifty record that is worth noting, though we will never know if it was intentional.

In early 1845, a fairly obscure figure named William P. Richards wrote to council member George Miller proposing a "Mormon Reserve" (a dedicated area where Mormons would be confined) as a solution to the ongoing conflict between Mormons and their neighbors in Illinois. To me, Richards comes across as meddling, tedious, and a bit self-congratulatory. Council members expressed some initial interest in the proposal, though it is not clear that their interest was genuine. They may have only wanted to buy themselves more time to finish the temple. At one point in the correspondence between Richards and Miller, Richards gave permission that the exchanges

The extant council minutes for March 10, 11, 13, and 14, 1844, were reconstructed in fall 1844 by William Clayton, based on journal entries, memory, and perhaps other records. Photograph by Welden C. Andersen. Courtesy of Church History Library, Salt Lake City.

be published in the newspaper but asked that the printer "guard against typographical errors."[29] When Clayton hand copied the correspondence into the record, however, he misspelled a word, making Richards's request a kind of joke on itself: "Please also *gaurd* against typographical errors."[30] In the rest of the record, Clayton spells "guard" or "guarded" correctly about ten times, with no other misspellings. While the misspelling "gaurd" could have resulted from the mere slip of a pen, one wonders if Clayton felt a bit exasperated at Richards's officiousness and decided to play a quiet trick on him.

INFORMATION ABOUT OTHER RECORDS

The Council of Fifty record provides a treasure trove of information about records (in addition to the minutes themselves) that were created, received, or reviewed by the council. On its website, the project has published a comprehensive list of such records, totaling roughly six dozen items.[31] We see in the volume and variety of these records a Church leadership who are coming of age in using the written word or published records to share information, to try to persuade others, to seek advice, to make decisions, and to document their history.

Besides all that we can infer about Mormon record keeping from Clayton's record, there is also some explicit commentary about the scope and purpose of the Church's flagship record-keeping project of that time. In a council meeting on March 22, 1845, discussion ensued about what kind of information was appropriate to include in the manuscript Church history then being compiled (the history was published serially in Church newspapers and then by B. H. Roberts as *History of the Church*). Willard Richards, one of those working on the history, asked whether all of the activities of the Nauvoo City Council should be included—"or only those in which pres^t J. Smith was particularly active in getting up."

Two other questions that arose in the discussion have probably been asked by many practicing Latter-day Saints today who write or publish Mormon history. To generalize: Do we leave out information that could be potentially embarrassing to a Church leader? And, How much information do we include about the activities of the Church's opponents? Joseph Smith provided the answer that would guide the history writers of that era: "He said if he was writing the history he should put in every thing which was valuable and leave out the rest." William W. Phelps also remarked in the discussion that Joseph Smith had earlier instructed him to put "every thing that was good" into the history.[32]

Willard Richards's suggestion that the level of Joseph Smith's involvement be the determining factor in questions of scope resonates to our own time, as the same factor is used by Joseph Smith Papers Project scholars to decide what to include in the comprehensive edition. The basic question is, Is this a Joseph Smith document (that is, was the record either created by him or received by him and kept in his office)? That question is dispositive, with no consideration of whether the content is "valuable" or "good." The underlying assumption is that publishing Joseph Smith's complete documentary record is of inherent value, a point with which William Clayton might have agreed.

NOTES

1. The council was formally organized March 11, 1844. The March 10 meeting can be considered a preliminary meeting of the council.

2. See Council of Fifty, Minutes, March 11 and 14, 1844; February 4, 1845; March 4, 1845, in Matthew J. Grow, Ronald K. Esplin, Mark Ashurst-McGee, Gerrit J. Dirkmaat, and Jeffrey D. Mahas, eds., *Council of Fifty, Minutes, March 1844–January 1846*, vol. 1 of the Administrative Records series of *The Joseph Smith Papers,* ed. Ronald K. Esplin, Matthew J. Grow, and Matthew C. Godfrey (Salt Lake City: Church Historian's Press, 2016), 42–43, 50, 224–25, 277 (hereafter *JSP,* CFM); Source Note and Historical Introduction to Council of Fifty, Minutes, in *JSP,* CFM:5–6, 8–14; George Q. Cannon to Joseph F. Smith, December 8, 1880, Church History Library, Salt Lake City.

3. See Andrew H. Hedges, Alex D. Smith, and Brent M. Rogers, eds., *Journals, Volume 3: May 1843–June 1844,* vol. 3 of the Journals series of *The Joseph Smith Papers*, ed. Ronald K. Esplin and Matthew J. Grow (Salt Lake City: Church Historian's Press, 2015) (hereafter *JSP,* J3). This volume contains numerous references to the Nauvoo council minutes. See, for example, *JSP,* J3:xvi.

4. See Source Note to Revelation Book 1, in Robin Scott Jensen, Robert J. Woodford, and Steven C. Harper, eds., *Revelations and Translations, Volume 1: Manuscript Revelation Books,* vol. 1 of the Revelations and Translations series of *The Joseph Smith Papers,* ed. Dean C. Jessee, Ronald K. Esplin, and Richard Lyman Bushman (Salt Lake City: Church Historian's Press, 2011), 4–5 (hereafter *JSP,* R1); Source Note to Joseph Smith, Journal, December 1841–December 1842, in Andrew H. Hedges, Alex D. Smith, and Richard Lloyd Anderson, eds., *Journals, Volume 2: December 1841–April 1843,* vol. 2 of the Journals series of *The Joseph Smith Papers,* ed. Dean C. Jessee, Ronald K. Esplin, and Richard Lyman Bushman (Salt Lake City: Church Historian's Press, 2011), 5 (hereafter *JSP,* J2); and Source Notes to Joseph Smith, History, Drafts, 1838–circa 1841, in Karen Lynn Davidson, David J. Whittaker, Mark Ashurst-McGee, and Richard L. Jensen, eds., *Histories, Volume 1: Joseph Smith Histories, 1832–1844,* vol. 1 of the Histories series of *The Joseph Smith Papers,* ed. Dean C. Jessee, Ronald K. Esplin, and Richard Lyman Bushman (Salt Lake City: Church Historian's Press, 2012), 187, 192.

5. "Substitute Words in the 1835 and 1844 Editions of the Doctrine and Covenants," in Robin Scott Jensen, Richard E. Turley Jr., and Riley M. Lorimer, eds.,

Revelations and Translations, Volume 2: Published Revelations, vol. 2 of the Revelations and Translations series of *The Joseph Smith Papers*, ed. Dean C. Jessee, Ronald K. Esplin, and Richard Lyman Bushman (Salt Lake City: Church Historian's Press, 2011), 708.

6. See, for example, Joseph Smith, Journal, March 4, 1843, in *JSP*, J2:297.

7. *JSP*, J3:200–201. Richards first wrote out the correct words, then came back later to cross them out and write them in backward, suggesting he had become worried about confidentiality sometime later. In this same journal passage, Richards also wrote and then later canceled the sentence "Joseph enquired perfect secrecy of them."

8. Council of Fifty, Minutes, March 14, 1844, in *JSP*, CFM:50.

9. Enos 1:13, 16; 3 Nephi 23:7–13; Doctrine and Covenants 21:1.

10. Record of the Twelve, February 27, 1835, 1–3; Minute Book 1, February 27, 1835, 86–88, both at josephsmithpapers.org.

11. Historical Introduction to Council of Fifty, Minutes, in *JSP*, CFM:13–14.

12. William Clayton, Journal, quoted in *JSP*, CFM:198n625; Events of June 1844, in *JSP*, CFM:197–98.

13. D. Michael Quinn, "The Council of Fifty and Its Members, 1844 to 1945," *BYU Studies* 20, no. 2 (1980): 192.

14. Council of Fifty, Minutes, March 10, 1844, in *JSP*, CFM:39.

15. Historical Introduction to Council of Fifty, Minutes, in *JSP*, CFM:7.

16. Council of Fifty, Minutes, April 5, 1844; May 3, 6, and 13, 1844, in *JSP*, CFM:81–82, 137, 148, 160. One may wonder whether Richards's minute-taking habits were different enough from Clayton's that the differences can be seen in the resulting minutes. Since we have only Clayton's fair copy of the minutes and none of the original raw minutes for these 1844 meetings, the question may be impossible to answer. (Given how difficult Richards's idiosyncratic handwriting is to transcribe, that any raw council minutes he kept did not survive may have been a boon to the Joseph Smith Papers team!) There is one meeting reported in the record, the one held February 27, 1845, at which neither Clayton nor Richards took the original minutes. Church scribe Thomas Bullock, not a member of the council, attended the meeting and took the minutes. (Editorial Note to Council of Fifty, Minutes, February 27, 1845, in *JSP*, CFM:247.)

17. Historical Introduction to Council of Fifty, Minutes, in *JSP*, CFM:11–14.

18. A common practice with many of the Church's records was to create original records on loose paper, then to transfer those into a permanent record book.

Revelation Book 1, Revelation Book 2, Minute Book 1, and Minute Book 2 (all available at josephsmithpapers.org) are examples.

19. Historical Introduction to Council of Fifty, Minutes, in *JSP*, CFM:9.

20. Andrew F. Ehat's 1980 article on the Council of Fifty includes transcripts of William Clayton's journal entries related to the Nauvoo council. Journal entries for the following dates note that Clayton was "copying" or "recording" the minutes of the council (meaning, copying and expanding the raw minutes into the fair copy): August 18, 1844; September 6, 1844; February 6, 11, 12, 1845; March 6, 7, [unknown day], 12, 14, 15, 17, 19, 20, 24, 27, 1845; April 1, 16, 17, 21, 22, 24, 28, 1845; September 11, 1845; October 5, 1845. These entries often note that the copying efforts took "all day." Andrew F. Ehat, "'It Seems Like Heaven Began on Earth': Joseph Smith and the Constitution of the Kingdom of God," *BYU Studies* 20, no. 3 (1980): 266–73.

21. *JSP*, R1:5.

22. Source Note and Historical Introduction to Minute Book 2, at josephsmith papers.org.

23. See Source Notes and Historical Introductions at josephsmithpapers.org for Joseph Smith Letterbook 2; Minute Book 2; and Joseph Smith, History, 1838–56, vol. A-1, respectively.

24. Joseph Smith, History, 1838–56, vol. C-1, 1260, at josephsmithpapers.org.

25. See editorial notes on and minutes of these meetings in *JSP*, CFM:19–50.

26. Council of Fifty, Minutes, April 18, 1844, in *JSP*, CFM:128.

27. Council of Fifty, Minutes, May 25, 1844, in *JSP*, CFM:169.

28. Historical Introduction to Council of Fifty, Minutes, in *JSP*, CFM:12–13.

29. William P. Richards to George Miller, February 3, 1845, Brigham Young Office Files, Church History Library, Salt Lake City.

30. Council of Fifty, Minutes, February 4, 1845, in *JSP*, CFM:216–18, 232–44; emphasis added.

31. "Documents Generated, Reviewed, and Received by the Council of Fifty in Nauvoo," at josephsmithpapers.org.

32. Council of Fifty, Minutes, March 22, 1845, in *JSP*, CFM:366–69.

Chapter 9

"TO CARRY OUT JOSEPH'S MEASURES IS SWEETER TO ME THAN HONEY"

Brigham Young and the Council of Fifty[1]

Matthew J. Grow and Marilyn Bradford

Seven months after the death of Joseph Smith, Brigham Young reconvened the Council of Fifty. Indicating his view of the council and his own role in succeeding Smith as chairman, Young stated that he intended to "have the priviledge of carrying out Josephs measures." Indeed, he continued, "To carry out Josephs measures is sweeter to me than the honey or the honey comb." Young hoped to enact the plans and priorities of Joseph Smith, who had established the Council of Fifty to "go and establish a Theocracy either in Texas or Oregon or somewhere in California" and to work "for the safety and salvation of the saints by protecting them in their religious rights and worship."[2]

After the council's reorganization, council member Orson Spencer cautioned Young, suggesting that he would also have to divert from Smith's policies: "When Joseph was here he was for carrying out his (Josephs) measures, he now wants pres^t Young as our head to carry out his own measures, and he believes they will be right whether they differ from Josephs measures or not. Different circumstances require different measures."[3] This interchange between Young and Spencer, which occurred during one of the most difficult eras in Mormon history, illustrates Young's dilemma: as the successor to Joseph Smith as leader of the Latter-day Saints, how to implement Smith's vision while also retaining flexibility as new circumstances arose.

Though the minutes of the Council of Fifty were published as part of *The Joseph Smith Papers*, they arguably provide more insight into Brigham Young than Joseph Smith. During the era of the Nauvoo minutes, March 1844–January 1846, the council operated for a much longer period of time under Young than Smith—with meetings spanning eleven months for Young versus three for Smith. In addition, the minutes of the Young era tend to be much more detailed, capturing more of Young's thoughts and the dynamics of the council. In fact, nearly 70 percent of the words in the Nauvoo minutes concern the Young era rather than the Smith era. Other records illustrating Young's work as an administrator—such as minutes from the Quorum of the Twelve—also tend to be more fragmentary than the council's minutes. As such, the council's minutes give rich insights into Young's personality, leadership style, and priorities.

YOUNG AND THE COUNCIL UNDER JOSEPH SMITH

Young was a member of the Council of Fifty during its entire existence in Nauvoo. Along with Smith and Willard Richards, Young was one of the addressees of the letters sent from Saints in Wisconsin Territory that served as the catalyst to organize the council. At the organizational meeting of the council, Young is listed after only Joseph and Hyrum Smith among the members, an indication of the increasing importance of his role as president of the Quorum of the Twelve Apostles.[4] Young recorded in his journal, "Met in councel at Br. J. Smith store in company a bout 20 to orginise our Selves into a compacked Boddy for the futher advenment of the gospel of Christ."[5]

Young appears to have spoken infrequently to the council at first, though the brief minutes of the opening meetings could obscure some of his participation. According to the records, he first spoke on March 21, when he seconded a motion from Joseph Smith that Erastus Snow serve a mission in Vermont.[6] Over the coming weeks, he became increasingly involved in making or seconding motions to the council, though he was not appointed to participate in any of the committees of the council.

During the first three months of the council, the minutes record two significant statements from Young, the first on April 5 and the second on April 18. In these remarks, Young articulated many themes that he would

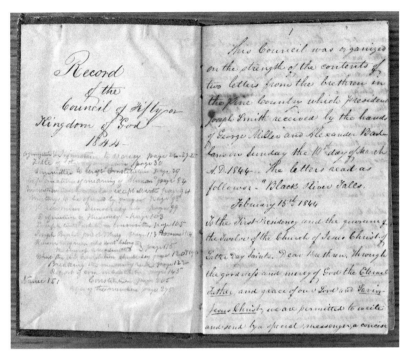

Brigham Young was an addressee of the February 15, 1844, letters that led to the formation of the Council of Fifty. Photograph by Welden C. Andersen. Courtesy of Church History Library, Salt Lake City.

return to in future council meetings and that defined some of his core beliefs as a leader of the Church, including the necessity of revelation and prophetic leadership, the merging of Church and state (particularly as seen in Utah during the first decade of settlement), and the emphasis on individual freedom and autonomy.[7]

In these statements, Young emphasized the primacy of revelation over written laws, telling the council that he "thought when he came in this church he should never want to keep book accounts again, Why? He thought the law would be written in every mans heart, and there would be that perfection in our lives, nothing further would be needed." Furthermore, he stated, "Revelations must govern. The voice of God, shall be the voice of the people." According to Young, revelation was suited to a particular moment in time. He stated that he "supposed there has not yet been a perfect revelation given, because we cannot understand it, yet we receive a little here and a little there."

Young would "not be stumbled if the prophet should translate the bible forty thousand times over and yet it should be different in some places every time, because when God speake, he always speaks according to the capacity of the people." In addition, Young taught that revelation would come after the people had done all they could: "When we had done all we were capable to do, we could have the Lord speak and tell us what is right." Obeying God's revelations would lead to further revelation: "When God sees that his people have enlarged upon what he has given us he will give us more."[8]

Young also spoke of his views of Joseph Smith and of prophets in general. "God appointed him," Young told the council. "We did not appoint him." As such, Smith in his role as a revelator could "disagree with the whole church" because he "is a perfect committee of himself." Indeed, Young stated, "It is the prerogative of the Almighty to differ from his subjects in what he pleases, or how, or when he pleases, and what will they do; they must bow to it, or kick themselves to death, or to hell." However, Young continued, "If it was necessary, and we were where we could not get at the prophet, we could get the revelations of the Lord straight."[9]

Young's statements also indicated his vision of earthly governments as compared with the kingdom of God. He recalled the "exalted views" he felt at the first meeting of the council when Smith "stated that this was the commencement of the organization of the kingdom of God." Though the kingdom of God was then just "in embryo," Young believed that it would "send forth its influence throughout the nations" and the governments of the world would sink "into oblivion." He gave his opinion that there was no distinction between the spiritual and the temporal: "No line can be drawn between the church and other governments, of the spiritual and temporal affairs of the church." Joseph Smith, by contrast, saw a distinction between the "Church of God and kingdom of God," asserting that the Church would govern in ecclesiastical matters while the kingdom would govern in civil matters. Nevertheless, a year later, Young reiterated that he saw this distinction less clearly than Smith, stating that he would "defy any man to draw the line between the spiritual and temporal affairs in the kingdom of God."[10]

Finally, Young spoke of his strong belief in independence and autonomy: "Republicanism is, to enjoy every thing there is in heaven, earth or hell to be enjoyed, and not infringe upon the rights of another." Later in 1844, William Smith referred to the "Mormon Creed" as "mind your own business." That statement resonated with Young, who often repeated it during his long ministry. "To mind your own business," Young later said, "incorporates the whole duty of man."[11]

Young's personality also comes through in these early council meetings. Known for the quality of his singing voice, Brigham often sang in public. One participant on the Camp of Israel (also known as Zion's Camp) in 1834, Levi Hancock, recalled that Brigham's duets with his brother Joseph "were the sweetest I ever heard in the Camps of Zion."[12] On four occasions in April and May, Young sang a parody of the popular patriotic song "Hail Columbia" that had been composed by council member William W. Phelps. In addition, Young was evidently among the council members who were excused in the afternoon session of April 25 because they were performing in a popular German play—*Pizarro; or, The Death of Rolla*—that evening. Young also showed his ability to think quickly. On April 11, Joseph Smith became so animated while speaking on worldly and heavenly constitutions that he broke a two-foot ruler in half. Young quipped, "As the rule was broken in the hands of our chairman so might every tyrannical government be broken before us."[13]

Young attended his last meeting of the council under Joseph Smith on May 6, after which he departed on an electioneering mission. He was in Peterborough, New Hampshire, when he received confirmation on July 16, 1844, that Joseph Smith had been killed. After gathering other apostles in the East, Young raced back to Nauvoo, where he and the other members of the Quorum of the Twelve took firm control over the Church organization. He continued many of the "measures of Joseph" over these months but did not immediately reorganize the Council of Fifty.[14]

REORGANIZATION OF THE COUNCIL

On February 4, 1845, after receiving news that the Illinois legislature had revoked the Nauvoo municipal charter, the Council of Fifty met for the first time following Smith's death. Young asked the other twenty-four men present "whether they are willing that I should take the place of brother Joseph as chairman." The men spoke in order of seniority. Samuel Bent, the oldest man, set the tone of the responses that followed: "He rejoices in the opportunity of meeting once more and feels steadfast in the principles and rules of the council as laid down by our beloved brother Joseph. He feels that it would be highly satisfactory to him to have president Young take the place of brother Joseph as chairman and carry out Josephs measures." Orson Pratt stated, "It is a thing selfevident that the president of the church stands at the head of this council." William Clayton said, "We cannot carry out Josephs measures but by sustaining Brigham Young as our chairman, our head and successor of Joseph Smith." Following the discussion, the council voted unanimously to sustain Young as "the standing chairman of this council and legal successor" to Smith. About a month later, council members unanimously received Young as "prophet, priest, and king to this kingdom forever after" as they had earlier received Joseph Smith.[15]

In addition to noting his own sustaining as leader of the council on February 4, Young reported in his journal that the council was "righted up & organized." That day, the council sustained as members the twenty-five men present and an additional fifteen men absent that day. Three men—including Joseph and Hyrum Smith—had died since the council's last meeting in May 1844. In addition, the council rejected eleven men on February 4, meaning that the membership stood at forty (fifty-four men had joined the council under Joseph Smith). The council dropped men seen as disloyal to Young and the Twelve Apostles, including Sidney Rigdon. While Young worked to reclaim individuals whose loyalty was in doubt—such as council members Lyman Wight and James Emmett, both of whom had led companies of Saints from Nauvoo over the objections of Young—he also did not want them in a confidential council.[16]

The council also dropped the three non-Mormons who had joined the council under Joseph Smith. It does not appear that the council rejected the men simply because they were non-Mormons. Of the three, one had been arrested for counterfeiting, one had been accused of threatening to "bring a mob on the church" around the time of Joseph Smith's murder, and the third later recalled that he had a falling-out with the Saints after Smith's death. However, no efforts were made to add any non-Mormons to the council. Rather, they were replaced—as were the other council members who had been dropped—by trusted Latter-day Saints over the next several weeks.[17]

HOW YOUNG OPERATED THE COUNCIL

The Council of Fifty met under Young's direction in Nauvoo from February through May 1845 and then, following a summer recess, from September 1845 through January 1846. Young later reconvened the council in Winter Quarters and then in territorial Utah. The detailed council minutes in 1845 and early 1846 give insights into Young's leadership approach for the thirty years that he led the Saints, including his stated reliance on revelation, his sometimes harsh rhetoric, and his focus on settlement and the temple. Young clearly felt the heavy weight of leading the Latter-day Saints during a perilous time. In describing his responsibility, he stated, "If men are set to lead a people it is not for them to consult and satisfy their own private feelings, but to use all the stratagem and cunning they are capable of to save the people."[18]

In leading the council, Young referred both to his ability to receive revelation to guide the Latter-day Saints and his belief that Joseph Smith had established the agenda they should follow. "While Joseph was living," he recalled, "it seems as though he was hurried by the Lord all the time, and especially for the last year." In Young's mind, "It seemed he laid out work for this church which would last them twenty years to carry out." At the same time, Young was confident that he and the other apostles could carry the work forward: "When the Twelve have been separated from Joseph in England or the Eastern States or elswhere, I defy any man to point out the time when I was in the dark in regard to what should be done. . . . Some have been fearful that I would blunder in the dark but it is not so." Other council members concurred. As Alpheus Cutler told the council in early May, "The only thing he wants is the word of Lord on the subject. . . . We have got a leader that can tell the mind of the Lord."[19]

Following the example of Joseph Smith, Young encouraged robust debate and discussion among council members. According to Young, "Joseph declared for every man to spue [spew] out every thing there was in him, and see if there is not a foundation in him for a great work. . . . He wants to hear the brethrens views on the subject, and by talking over each others views, we learn each others feelings, and all learn what each other knows." Certainly, Young stated, "There has always been an objection in this church to listening to what is term explateration [a slang term meaning to explain in detail], but if there are fools amongst us let them speak out their

Brigham Young reorganized the Council of Fifty on February 4, 1845. Daguerre-otype, circa 1846, attributed to Lucian R. Foster. Courtesy of Church History Library, Salt Lake City.

folly, and we will know who are men of wisdom." Like Smith, Young also presided over the council through parliamentary procedure and the establishment of committees. According to Young, running the council both by revelation and candid debate meant that it was a "living body to enact laws for the government of this kingdom, we are a living constitution."[20]

While Young encouraged vigorous discussions, his opinions and decisions—like those of Joseph Smith the previous year—held enormous sway. For instance, on March 22, after six weeks of discussions on a proposal to send missionaries to American Indian tribes, Orson Spencer motioned that Young make final decisions. Young initially "objected inasmuch as the responsibility rests upon the council." In response, George Miller stated that the council had thoroughly discussed the matter and that he was "in favor of immediate action, and dont want to see the ship rot on the stocks." Young then agreed to move forward as the final decision maker.[21] On other topics, council members likewise indicated that Young should make decisions following discussion.

One difference between the Joseph Smith era and the Brigham Young era was that under Young, the Quorum of the Twelve Apostles became more important to the Council of Fifty. On April 11, Young stated, "Formerly one man stood at the head, now the Twelve stand there." Over time, Young sometimes relied on prior discussions among the Twelve before meetings of the Council of Fifty to make decisions in the council. For instance, at the April 11, 1845, meeting, the Council of Fifty endorsed decisions regarding the Church's publishing program and the Nauvoo print shop that had been made the previous day by the Quorum of the Twelve.[22]

PRIORITIES OF THE COUNCIL UNDER YOUNG

Under Young's direction, the Council of Fifty engaged less in the wide-ranging debates about earthly and heavenly constitutions that occupied it under Joseph Smith. Rather, the council focused on more practical matters, particularly how to govern the Saints in and around Nauvoo following the loss of the municipal charter, exploration of relationships with American Indian tribes, a search for a sanctuary in the American West, and the completion of the Nauvoo Temple. The shift from the philosophical to the pragmatic reflected Young's own practical personality. In addition, the discussions under Smith had at least partially resolved many of the pressing theoretical concerns, such as the purpose of the council and the meaning of theocracy for the Latter-day Saints. Finally, the pragmatic turn under Young reflected the increasingly tenuous situation of the Latter-day Saints in Nauvoo: events demanded concrete decisions and a clear way forward for the Saints.

How to respond to the loss of the Nauvoo charter was of immediate concern when the council reconvened in February 1845. The Latter-day Saints had explicitly designed the charter to provide them with protections they had lacked in Missouri, including their own independent militia and municipal court with the unusual power of issuing writs of habeas corpus. The revocation of the charter—an indication that Illinois leaders believed the Mormons incapable of self-government—left the Mormons in Nauvoo without a city council, a court, a militia, a police force, and even the right to perform marriages. In the words of William Clayton, the revocation of the charter "laid us open to all the raviges of mobs & murderers." Without the charter, the Saints felt especially vulnerable to internal dissidents, criminals who would prey upon the populace, and even the threat of a concerted outside attack by their enemies.[23]

Over the next several months, the Council of Fifty essentially became a shadow government in Nauvoo as it explored ways either to fight the repeal of the charter or to provide a semblance of government for the city. For instance, Young and other members of the council sent letters to leading lawyers asking for recommendations to seek legal and judicial remedies. They also wrote letters to the governors of each US state asking for their response to Mormon persecution and about the prospect of the Latter-day Saints settling elsewhere. Young, though, had little hope, telling the council that "the only object of our writing to the governors is to give them the privilege of sealing their own damnation." On a more concrete level, the council helped establish an extralegal police force in the city—known as the "whistling and whittling brigades"—which relied on Church members to watch suspicious visitors to Nauvoo and, if necessary, intimidate them to leave the city. The council's minutes indicate that the Saints were responding to real threats and that, when the vigilante justice threatened to get out of hand, Young tightened the controls on it.[24]

Even as council members discussed ways to govern and protect Nauvoo, they became increasingly focused on leaving the city. In 1844, the council had explored various possibilities for possible western settlements, focusing on California, Oregon, and Texas, all of which were then outside the borders of the United States. When council members learned that Texas had been annexed to the United States in March 1845, they no longer saw it as a viable option. Similarly, Oregon eventually dropped out of consideration, leading Young and other members of the council to increasingly focus on the Mexican territories that covered much of what is now the western United States. On March 1, Young instructed the council, "The time has come when we must seek out a location." He connected the need for a sanctuary to the deteriorating situation for the Latter-day Saints in Illinois and the rest of the United States: "The yoke of the gentiles is broke, their doom is sealed, there is not the least fibre can possibly be discovered that binds us to the gentile world."[25]

The early months of 1845 were dark days for Young and other Church leaders, as they contemplated the loss of the Nauvoo charter, feared the possibility that they would be driven from Illinois as they had from Missouri, and worried that Church leaders would be arrested on judicial writs from false charges, as they believed Joseph and Hyrum Smith had been the previous year. In response to his concerns, Young advocated that missionary work cease to the "Gentiles"—whom Young perceived as white Americans and Europeans—and focus rather on the house of Israel, including American Indians and others. Young also instructed at this time that the Relief Society not reconvene, as it had the previous two springs, apparently believing that some members had used the Relief Society to foment opposition against plural marriage and Joseph Smith.[26]

Young's concern can also be seen in his increasingly harsh rhetoric within the Council of Fifty. Believing that "the gentiles" had rejected the gospel, persecuted the Latter-day Saints in Missouri and Illinois, and murdered Joseph and Hyrum Smith, he said that he did not "care about preaching to the gentiles any longer." Paraphrasing Lyman Wight, he stated, "Let the damned scoundrels be killed, let them be swept off from the earth, and then we can go and be baptized for them, easier than we can convert them." Furthermore, Young vowed that he would not allow himself to be taken by what he viewed as corrupt judicial officers with false writs.[27]

Young's statements to the council regarding inflammatory speeches also give insight into his rhetoric. In March 1845, Young rebutted a comment that Almon Babbitt had made about Mormon rhetoric several years earlier in Missouri, a comment Young believed was targeted at Joseph Smith. "No man can ever speak against Joseph in my presence," Young stated, "but I shall tell him of it." Referencing those earlier speeches, which many believed had contributed to violence against the Saints, Young explained, "To the natural man this church has from the beginning had a boasting spirit but to the priesthood it does not appear so." According to Young, "A man never could speak by the power of the spirit but his language would appear to this ungodly world as inflammatory." Thus, Young partly attributed the inflammatory nature of some statements by himself and others as inspired by the Spirit. Nevertheless, a month later, Young also cautioned council members "to cease all kinds of harsh speeches which would cause the spirit of God to leave us. We want to lay aside all such things that we may enjoy peace in the city."[28]

Under Young, the Council of Fifty focused on the need for the Saints to find a sanctuary in the West. Besides sending emissaries to American Indians, council members also studied the latest maps and reports and explorations. As new information came in, the council eliminated possibilities they considered impractical. Eventually the council began to focus on the Rocky Mountains and then the valley of the Great Salt Lake as the destination. Throughout this process, council members felt that they were being guided by revelation, but not until the time for departure neared did Young feel confident of the exact destination. On January 13, 1846, as the Saints were preparing to leave their homes in Nauvoo, Young declared, "The Saying of the Prophets would never be verified unless the House of the Lord should be reared in the Tops of the Mountains & the Proud Banner of liberty wave over the valley's that are within the Mountains &c. I know where the spot is."[29]

Young's statement occurred when the Council of Fifty was meeting in the attic of the Nauvoo temple. Over the previous month, one of the council's objectives had been realized: the completion of enough of the Nauvoo temple so the Latter-day Saints could perform temple rituals before they left for the West. A year earlier, in January 1845, Young had contemplated whether the Saints should remain in Nauvoo until the completion of the temple. He sought in prayer an answer and recorded the response: "we should." On March 1, 1845, Young tied the completion of the temple with the exodus from Nauvoo: "It is for us to take care of ourselves and go and pick out a place where we can go and dwell in peace after we have finished the houses [the temple and the Nauvoo House] and got our endowment, not but that the Lord can give it to us in the wilderness, but I have no doubt we shall get it here." On November 30, 1845, the construction was far enough along that Young partially dedicated the temple, and temple ordinance work—particularly endowments and marriage sealings—began on December 10. It was thus fitting that the final work of the Council of Fifty in Nauvoo involved final preparations for the exodus as the council met in the temple. Only when he was standing in the temple, as endowments and sealings occurred in nearby rooms, could Brigham Young announce with clarity the final destination of the Latter-day Saints' exodus.[30]

NOTES

1. The language of this quotation has been standardized slightly for purposes of the title.

2. Council of Fifty, Minutes, March 1, 1845, March 11, 1844, April 18, 1844, in Matthew J. Grow, Ronald K. Esplin, Mark Ashurst-McGee, Gerrit J. Dirkmaat, and Jeffrey D. Mahas, eds., *Council of Fifty, Minutes, March 1844–January 1846*, vol. 1 of the Administrative Records series of *The Joseph Smith Papers*, ed. Ronald K. Esplin, Matthew J. Grow, and Matthew C. Godfrey (Salt Lake City: Church Historian's Press, 2016), 257, 40, 128 (hereafter *JSP*, CFM).

3. Council of Fifty, Minutes, February 4, 1845, in *JSP*, CFM:222.

4. Council of Fifty, Minutes, March 10 and 11, 1844, in *JSP*, CFM:32, 36, 43.

5. Brigham Young, Journal, March 13, 1844, Church History Library, Salt Lake City.

6. Council of Fifty, Minutes, March 21, 1844, in *JSP*, CFM:59.

7. Council of Fifty, Minutes, April 5 and 18, 1844, in *JSP*, CFM:82–84, 119–21.

8. Council of Fifty, Minutes, April 5 and 18, 1844, in *JSP*, CFM:82, 119.

9. Council of Fifty, Minutes, April 18, 1844, in *JSP*, CFM:120–21.

10. Council of Fifty, Minutes, April 18, 1844, April 5, 1844, April 11, 1845, in *JSP*, CFM:119, 82, 128, 401.

11. Council of Fifty, Minutes, April 5, 1844, in *JSP*, CFM:84; Michael Hicks, "Minding Business: A Note on 'The Mormon Creed,'" *BYU Studies Quarterly* 26, no. 4 (Fall 1986): 128; Brigham Young, Discourse, May 15, 1864, *Journal of Discourses* (Liverpool: F. D. Richards, 1855–86), 10:295.

12. Leonard Arrington, *American Moses* (Urbana: University of Illinois Press, 1986), 40.

13. Council of Fifty, Minutes, April 18, 1844, May 3, 1844, April 25, 1844, April 11, 1844, in *JSP*, CFM:110, 118, 138, 131, 101.

14. Council of Fifty, Minutes, May 6, 1844, in *JSP*, CFM:147–59; "Part 2: February–May 1845," in *JSP*, CFM:205.

15. Council of Fifty, Minutes, February 4, 1845, March 1, 1845, in *JSP*, CFM:218–25, 256.

16. Young, Journal, February 4, 1845; Council of Fifty, Minutes, February 4, 1845, in *JSP*, CFM:216, 225–27.

17. Council of Fifty, Minutes, February 4, 1845, in *JSP*, CFM:226–27.

18. Council of Fifty, Minutes, May 6, 1845, in *JSP*, CFM:448.

19. Council of Fifty, Minutes, March 1, 1845, May 6, 1845, in *JSP*, CFM:257, 445.

20. Council of Fifty, Minutes, April 11, 1845, March 1, 1845, in *JSP*, CFM:254, 401.

21. Council of Fifty, Minutes, March 22, 1845, in *JSP*, CFM:353–56.

22. Council of Fifty, Minutes, April 11, 1845, in *JSP*, CFM:390, 398.

23. "Part 2: February–May 1845," in *JSP*, CFM:212–15; William Clayton, Journal, December 27, 1844, quoted in *JSP*, CFM:213.

24. Council of Fifty, Minutes, March 11, 1845, March 18, 1845, in *JSP*, CFM:312, 330–31.

25. "Volume Introduction," in *JSP*, CFM:xlii; Council of Fifty, Minutes, March 1, 1845, in *JSP*, CFM:257.

26. Document 1.13, in Jill Mulvay Derr, Carol Cornwall Madsen, Kate Holbrook, and Matthew J. Grow, *The First Fifty Years of Relief Society: Key Documents in Latter-day Saint Women's History* (Salt Lake City: Church Historian's Press, 2016), 168–71.

27. Council of Fifty, Minutes, March 11, 1845, March 18, 1845, April 15, 1845, in *JSP*, CFM:299–300, 337, 424–25.

28. Council of Fifty, Minutes, March 11, 1845, April 15, 1845, in *JSP*, CFM:307–9, 421–22.

29. John D. Lee, Journal, January 13, 1846, 79.

30. Council of Fifty, Minutes, January 13, 1846, March 1, 1845, in *JSP*, CFM:257–58, 521; Young, Journal, January 24, 1845; "Part 4: January 1846," in *JSP*, CFM:507.

Chapter 10

AMERICAN INDIANS AND THE NAUVOO-ERA COUNCIL OF FIFTY

Jeffrey D. Mahas

"We'll ask our cousin Lemuel, to join us heart & hand,
And spread abroad our curtains, throughout fair Zions land"

John Taylor, April 11, 1845[1]

Most scholarship on the Council of Fifty has focused on the political and religious aspirations of the council and its members. Questions of theo-democracy, Joseph Smith's presidential campaign, or westward migration have dominated these discussions.[2] With the publication of the minutes of the council by the Joseph Smith Papers Project, it is clear that historians have underestimated the degree to which perceptions of and plans related to American Indians played into the Council of Fifty's actions in Nauvoo.[3] Indeed, the council's discussions during 1845 largely revolved around designs to establish alliances with and among the Indians living west of the Mississippi River. These discussions in the Council of Fifty reveal the central role Mormons assigned to Indians as they planned for their westward migration.

Mormon interest in American Indians originated with the Book of Mormon, which principally narrates the story of two civilizations: the Nephites and the Lamanites. According to Book of Mormon prophecies, the descendants of the Lamanites—identified by early Mormons as all Native Americans—would receive the Book of Mormon and convert en masse to the faith their forefathers had rejected. The Lamanites would then scourge all those who refused to repent "as a lion among the beasts of the forest, as a young lion among the flocks of sheep" before joining with the repentant Gentiles—the Mormon designation for white Euro-Americans—in building a New Jerusalem in North America.[4] Both the Book of Mormon and Joseph Smith's later revelations associated the mass conversion of the Lamanites and the subsequent conflict with the beginning of the Millennium.[5]

During the 1830s and early 1840s, Mormons made several attempts to bring about the conversion of the Lamanites, starting with the September 1830 commission directing Oliver Cowdery to "go unto the Lamanites & Preach my Gospel unto them & cause my Church to be established among them."[6] During the 1830s, rumors of Mormon-Indian alliances among the Saints' non-Mormon neighbors fueled anti-Mormon accusations and violence.[7] Within a few years, Church leaders encouraged members to downplay Mormon interest toward Indians.[8] The 1840s saw a return to proselytizing among American Indians, with men such as Jonathan Dunham, James Emmett, and John Lowe Butler being sent to the Stockbridge, Potawatomi, Sioux, and others groups in the Indian Territory west of the Missouri River or elsewhere. However, the purposes or expectations of these missions were shrouded in secrecy.[9] One of the great contributions of the Council of Fifty's minutes is that they provide a more detailed explanation of early Mormon expectations for American Indians than previously existed, especially for 1844 and 1845.

THE COUNCIL OF FIFTY UNDER JOSEPH SMITH

Indians played a crucial role in the immediate impetus for the organization of the council. In 1843, apostle Lyman Wight and bishop George Miller led a large company of Saints to Black River Falls, Wisconsin Territory, to continue the Church's lumber operations in the region.[10] During the following winter, these Saints had frequent contact with Winnebago, Chippewa, and Menominee Indians and sought permission to begin missionary work among these tribes.[11] Before they could follow through

Joseph Smith conferred with a number of American Indian delegations in Nauvoo in the 1840s. Lithograph by Henry R. Robinson based on drawing probably by Edward W. Clay. *Joseph the Prophet Addressing the Lamanites* (New York City: Prophet, 1844). Courtesy of Church History Library, Salt Lake City.

with their intentions, a hostile federal Indian agent in the area mistakenly claimed that the Mormons were trespassing on Menominee Indian lands, and local Mormon leaders began to worry that they would be forced from the area. Rather than return to Nauvoo, these men, led by Wight and Miller, wrote to Joseph Smith, proposing that the Wisconsin Saints abandon their logging efforts and instead create a Mormon colony in the Republic of Texas. They claimed with a great deal of exaggeration that the local Indians had received the Mormons "as their councilors both temporal and spiritual" and that they could convince these Indians to come with them to Texas. There they could create a settlement that would provide a foothold to spread the gospel to the native peoples in western North America as well as in Central and South America.[12]

When Joseph Smith received the letters on March 10, he assembled a small group of trusted Church leaders and advisers that would quickly become the Council of Fifty to discuss the Wisconsin Saints' proposal. Despite the enthusiasm contained in these letters, American Indians were never the primary focus of the Council of Fifty under Smith's leadership. Instead, the council focused much of its attention on the Wisconsin Saints' proposal for a Mormon colony in the Republic of Texas.

On January 1, 1845, William Clayton, the council's clerk, reflected on the council's activities for the previous year and wrote that the council had "devised [a plan] to restore the Ancients [i.e., Indians] to the Knowledge of the truth and the restoration of Union and peace amongst ourselves."[13] Nevertheless, under Joseph Smith, the council's only explicit action in the minutes was to follow up on the Wisconsin Saints' exaggerated reports by sending James Emmett "on a mission to the Lamanites [in Wisconsin] to instruct them to unite together," presumably in preparation for their eventual mass conversion.[14] When Emmett conveyed his message to a Menominee leader, possibly Chief Oshkosh, the leader largely dismissed its practicality, and Emmett returned with nothing to show for his efforts.[15] Additionally, on April 4, the Council of Fifty met with a delegation of Potawatomi Indians in Nauvoo and Joseph Smith encouraged the visitors to "cease their wars with each other."[16]

While the Council of Fifty spent little time in 1844 discussing or contemplating how Indians would fit into this new millenarian government, their attitudes changed after Joseph Smith was killed by an anti-Mormon lynch mob on June 27, 1844. In the Mormon worldview, Smith's violent death was a literal and total rejection of the Mormons and their message by the nation. Smith's death eroded whatever positive feelings remained for the United States among the Mormons. When the Illinois legislature repealed the statute providing a city government for Nauvoo in January 1845, it added to their outrage. Mormons interpreted these major disappointments within their millenarian worldview, associating their setbacks with the plight of Native peoples. Brigham Young publicly preached that the actions of Illinois and the United States had expelled the Mormons from political citizenship and made them "a distinct nation just as much as the Lamanites."[17] Given this state of affairs, many Mormons now believed that the promised time had come for the American Indians to convert and "vex the Gentiles with a soar vexation."[18]

THE COUNCIL OF FIFTY UNDER BRIGHAM YOUNG

With Mormons already interpreting recent setbacks within their millenarian framework, their worldview was seemingly confirmed with the unannounced and unexpected arrival in Nauvoo of Lewis Dana on January 27, 1845. Dana—a member of the Oneida nation—had been baptized along with his wife and daughter in the spring of 1840 after Dimick Huntington read them the entire Book of Mormon over the course of two or three weeks.[19] Several Mormons, including apostle Wilford Woodruff, interpreted Dana's conversion as the beginning of the prophesied redemption of the Lamanites.[20] When Dana returned to Nauvoo in 1845, Latter-day Saints began again to discuss his place in the millennial Mormon–American Indian alliance. In February, Dana received a prophetic statement known as a patriarchal blessing that stated he would be "a Mighty instrument in knitting the hearts of the Lamanites together . . . bringing thousands to a knowledge of their Redeemer & to a knowledge of their Fathers." The blessing explicitly connected Dana to the prophecies contained in the Book of Mormon, promising that he would "gather thousands of them [Lamanites] to the City of Zion."[21]

A week after Dana's arrival in Nauvoo, Brigham Young reconvened the Council of Fifty for the first time since Joseph Smith's death. While the repeal of the city charter in January 1845 forced Church leaders to reconsider plans to find a new home, Dana's arrival likely rekindled hopes that the other tasks charged to the council could be completed. Indeed, under Brigham Young the anticipated conversion of the American Indians took on a much more central role in the council's deliberations. Throughout February, Church leaders informally discussed the possible role Dana would play in their designs. On March 1, 1845, the Council of Fifty began discussing Dana's mission in earnest. At the beginning of the meeting, Young formally added Dana and nine other Mormons to the council—including Jonathan Dunham, a frequent missionary to the American Indians. When introducing Dana, Young told him that the council was organized not only "to find a place where we can dwell in peace and lift of the standard of liberty" but also "for the purpose of uniting the Lamanites, and sowing the seeds of the gospel among them. They will receive it en Masse." As the "first of the Lamanites" to be "admitted to this kingdom," Dana sensed his responsibility to bring about the long-anticipated mass conversion of his people and swore with uplifted hand, "In the name of the Lord I am willing to do all I can."[22]

At this meeting of the Council of Fifty, Young announced his intentions to send eight men west with Dana to go from tribe to tribe seeking to forge a pan-Indian alliance. "I want to see the Lamanites come in by thousands and the time has come," Young stated.[23] The certainty Young and other council members placed on an imminent Lamanite conversion reveals how thoroughly immersed they were in Mormonism's millenarian theology. "Our time is short among the gentiles, and the judgment of God will soon come on them like [a] whirlwind" Young declared on March 11, 1845.[24] The council seemed to universally agree that in light of recent events they should halt Mormon missionary efforts among the Euro-Americans they viewed as Gentiles. Following the private deliberations of the Council of Fifty, Young publicly announced on March 16 that he would "scarcely send a man out to preach" that year, stating that "if the world wants preachers, let them come here."[25] Young reiterated this policy a month later at the Church's general conference, reasoning that just as the ancient apostles turned to the Gentiles when the Jews rejected the gospel, the latter-day apostles would preach only to Israelites because the Gentiles had rejected the gospel.[26] Apostle Heber C. Kimball took this resolve one step further and encouraged a total separation from the Gentile world.

Contextually it is clear that the decision to not preach or interact with the Gentiles was directed solely toward white Americans and that Mormonism's missionary impulse remained intact, in theory, on a global scale.[27]

THE WESTERN MISSION

Nevertheless, the Mormons' more global ambitions were put on hold in favor of the immediate mission to the American Indians. While the Council of Fifty was unanimous in believing that the time had come to send a delegation to the Native peoples in the West, there was less agreement over how the missionaries should proceed. For nearly two months following Brigham Young's announcement of the mission, the body debated the missionaries' destination and message. By March 18, Jonathan Dunham had received intelligence that eventually helped settle these debates. On that day, Dunham announced that he had learned of "a council of the delegates of all the Indians Nations" that would take place in southern Indian Territory in the summer of 1845.[28]

The council Dunham described had been called by the Creeks in response to violent altercations with both the Pawnee and the Comanche. According to James Logan, the federal Indian agent to the Creeks, the council was to be "an assemblage of deputations from all the Indian Tribes on this frontier as well as those of the wandering tribes of the distant Prairies to meet in Council on the Deep Fork on the first of May next, with a view of settling all difficulties that may exist between them respectively, and to discuss such matters as may tend to advance peaceable and amicable relations."[29] Logan's description of the scope of this council was no exaggeration. According to the *Cherokee Advocate*, by May 1845 nearly 850 delegates from eleven tribes had assembled at the Creek council ground.[30]

It is unclear how Dunham learned of this impending Indian council; however, the Council of Fifty immediately made attendance at this pan-Indian council a central goal of the "Western Mission." Although Brigham Young had initially called for a party of eight or more, by April the council favored sending a smaller group of missionaries. On April 23, 1845, Lewis Dana and the men chosen to accompany him—Jonathan Dunham, Charles Shumway, and Phineas Young—left Nauvoo and began traveling southwest to the region surrounding Fort Leavenworth. There

The Council of Fifty dispatched Phineas Young and other "western missionaries" to attempt to forge alliances with American Indian tribes. Courtesy of Church History Library, Salt Lake City.

the missionaries tarried for ten days among the western Stockbridge and Kickapoo before continuing their journey south to the Indian council.[31] Both tribes had a history of favorable contact with Mormons, especially Dunham, and their interactions with the missionaries proved to be the only favorable results of the mission.[32] Unfortunately for the missionaries, their lengthy stay with the Stockbridge meant that the missionaries missed the conference they hoped to attend. Faced with this disappointment, Phineas Young and Charles Shumway abandoned the mission and returned to Nauvoo.[33] For his part, Phineas Young was disgusted with the whole affair and blamed the failures on Dana and Dunham's incompetence.[34]

Meanwhile, Dunham and Dana remained west of the Missouri in Indian Territory and reverted to the original plan of going tribe to tribe. In August, Brigham Young sent out another small wave of missionaries to the Indians, but when they arrived near Fort Leavenworth they were met by Dana and another Mormon Indian, who brought news that Dunham had died in late July after an illness of three weeks.[35] When the council heard a report on the missionary efforts in September 1845, Young sought to put a positive spin on their labors, claiming that they had now "learned considerable of the feelings of the Indians towards us, and the prospect is good."[36] Nevertheless, talk of an immediate Indian alliance disappeared from the council. While the missionaries had been gone, Church leaders had largely abandoned their more militaristic and millennial rhetoric surrounding a potential Mormon-Indian alliance. Under Brigham Young's direction, a select group of Church leaders had formulated a new plan to send a company of Saints west, "somewhere near the Great Salt Lake." In the fall and winter of 1845, the Council of Fifty primarily concerned itself with the practical preparations to move nearly fifteen thousand men, women, and children across the Rocky Mountains.[37]

Young optimistically looked to the West as the location for the promised redemption of the Lamanites to begin. Speaking of the Mormons' contemplated home on the other side of the Rocky Mountains just a month before their departure from Nauvoo, Young reasoned that "it is a place where we could get access to all the tribes on the northern continent and some of the tribes could be easily won over. The shoshows [Shoshones] are a numerous tribe and just as quick as we could give them a pair of breeches and a blanket they would be our servants, and cultivate the earth for us the year round."[38] Thus, the Mormon attempts to form an Indian alliance were deferred to await the removal of the Saints from Nauvoo and the colonization of the Great Basin.

CONCLUSION

Despite all the time and attention the Council of Fifty invested in bringing about the hoped-for conversion of and alliance with American Indians, they had had little or no success by the time wagons began crossing the Mississippi River in February 1846. Nevertheless, for historians interested in Mormon-Indian relations, the records of the council's deliberations provide an unprecedented window into Mormon expectations during the tumultuous years of 1844 to 1846. However, the value of the Council of Fifty minutes is not limited to the chronological scope of the minutes. Instead, the debates and discussions surrounding Mormon conceptions of and designs for American Indians illuminate earlier secretive attitudes and beliefs and also provide greater context for understanding the relationship between Mormon settlers and their Indian neighbors in the Great Basin through the nineteenth century and beyond.

NOTES

1. From Taylor's lyrics to the song "The Upper California," in Council of Fifty, Minutes, April 11, 1845, in Matthew J. Grow, Ronald K. Esplin, Mark Ashurst-McGee, Gerrit J. Dirkmaat, and Jeffrey D. Mahas, eds., *Council of Fifty, Minutes, March 1844–January 1846*, vol. 1 of the Administrative Records series of *The Joseph Smith Papers*, ed. Ronald K. Esplin, Matthew J. Grow, and Matthew C. Godfrey (Salt Lake City: Church Historian's Press, 2016), 402 (hereafter *JSP*, CFM).

2. See, for example, Klaus J. Hansen, *Quest for Empire: The Political Kingdom of God and the Council of Fifty in Mormon History* (East Lansing: Michigan State University Press, 1967); D. Michael Quinn, "The Council of Fifty and Its Members, 1844–1945," *BYU Studies* 20, no. 2 (Winter 1980): 163–97; Andrew F. Ehat, "'It Seems Like Heaven Began on Earth': Joseph Smith and the Constitution of the Kingdom of God," *BYU Studies* 20, no. 3 (Spring 1980): 253–80; and Jedediah S. Rogers, ed., *The Council of Fifty: A Documentary History* (Salt Lake City: Signature Books, 2014).

3. A slight exception may be scholarship focusing on Mormon splinter groups—such as the one led by Alpheus Cutler, who later placed a great deal of emphasis on Indian missions. See, for example, Danny L. Jorgensen, "Building the Kingdom of God: Alpheus Cutler and the Second Mormon Mission to the Indians, 1846–1853," *Kansas History* 15, no. 3 (Autumn 1992): 192–209.

4. 3 Nephi 21:12; Richard Lyman Bushman, *Joseph Smith: Rough Stone Rolling* (New York: Knopf, 2005), 84–108; W. Paul Reeve, *Religion of a Different Color: Race and the Mormon Struggle for Whiteness* (Oxford: Oxford University Press, 2015), 57–58; Armand L. Mauss, *All Abraham's Children: Changing Mormon Conceptions of Race and Lineage* (Urbana: University of Illinois, 2003), 48–52.

5. Revelation, December 25, 1832 [D&C 87], in Matthew C. Godfrey, Mark Ashurst-McGee, Grant Underwood, Robert J. Woodford, and William G. Hartley, eds., *Documents, Volume 2: July 1831–January 1833*, vol. 2 of the Documents series of *The Joseph Smith Papers*, ed. Dean C. Jessee, Ronald K. Esplin, Richard Lyman Bushman, and Matthew J. Grow (Salt Lake City: Church Historian's Press, 2013), 330–31 (hereafter *JSP*, D2); Revelation, December 16–17, 1833 [D&C 101], in Gerrit J. Dirkmaat, Brent M. Rogers, Grant Underwood, Robert J. Woodford, and William G. Hartley, eds., *Documents, Volume 3: February 1833–March 1834*, vol. 3 of the Documents series of *The Joseph Smith Papers*,

ed. Ronald K. Esplin and Matthew J. Grow (Salt Lake City: Church Historian's Press, 2014), 396.

6. Revelation, September 1830–B [D&C 28], in Michael Hubbard MacKay, Gerrit J. Dirkmaat, Grant Underwood, Robert J. Woodford, and William G. Hartley, eds., *Documents, Volume 1: July 1828–June 1831*, vol. 1 of the Documents series of *The Joseph Smith Papers,* ed. Dean C. Jessee, Ronald K. Esplin, Richard Lyman Bushman, and Matthew J. Grow (Salt Lake City: Church Historian's Press, 2013), 185.

7. Reeve, *Religion of a Different Color*, 52–105.

8. Joseph Smith to William W. Phelps, July 31, 1832, in *JSP*, D2:266.

9. Ronald W. Walker, "Seeking the 'Remnant': The Native American during the Joseph Smith Period," *Journal of Mormon History* 19, no. 1 (1993): 1–33.

10. George Miller to "Dear Brother," June 27, 1855, *Northern Islander*, August 23, 1855, [1].

11. See for example Joseph Smith, Journal, February 20, 1844, in Andrew H. Hedges, Alex D. Smith, and Brent M. Rogers, eds., *Journals, Volume 3: May 1843–June 1844*, vol. 3 of the Journals series of *The Joseph Smith Papers*, ed. Ronald K. Esplin and Matthew J. Grow (Salt Lake City: Church Historian's Press, 2015), 179.

12. Lyman Wight et al. to Joseph Smith et al., February 15, 1844; George Miller et al. to Joseph Smith et al., February 15, 1844, in *JSP*, CFM:17–39.

13. William Clayton, Journal, January 1, 1845, quoted in Ehat, "'It Seems Like Heaven Began on Earth,'" 268.

14. Council of Fifty, Minutes, March 21, 1844, in *JSP*, CFM:58.

15. Council of Fifty, Minutes, May 31, 1844, in *JSP*, CFM:171.

16. Council of Fifty, Minutes, April 4, 1844, in *JSP*, CFM:75–76.

17. William Clayton, Journal, February 26, 1845, quoted in James B. Allen, *No Toil nor Labor Fear: The Story of William Clayton*, Biographies in Latter-day Saint History (Provo, UT: Brigham Young University Press, 2002), 174.

18. Revelation, December 25, 1832 [D&C 87], in *JSP*, D2:330.

19. Oliver B. Huntington, History, 1845–46, 83, Oliver Boardman Huntington, Papers, 1843–1932, L. Tom Perry Special Collections, Harold B. Lee Library, Brigham Young University, Provo, UT.

20. Wilford Woodruff, Journal, July 13, 1840, in *Wilford Woodruff's Journal, 1833–1898*, ed. Scott G. Kenney, vol. 1, *1833–1840* (Midvale, UT: Signature Books, 1983), 483.

21. Patriarchal Blessing, John Smith to Lewis Dana, ca. 1845, Patriarchal Blessing Collection, Church History Library, Salt Lake City (hereafter CHL).

22. Council of Fifty, Minutes, March 1, 1845, in *JSP*, CFM:255.

23. Council of Fifty, Minutes, March 1, 1845, in *JSP*, CFM:257.

24. Council of Fifty, Minutes, March 11, 1845, in *JSP*, CFM:299.

25. Minutes, March 16, 1845, Historian's Office, General Church Minutes, 1839–1877, CHL.

26. "The Conference," *Nauvoo Neighbor*, April 16, 1845, [2].

27. Council of Fifty, Minutes, March 22, 1845, in *JSP*, CFM:356.

28. Council of Fifty, Minutes, March 18, 1845, in *JSP*, CFM:342.

29. James Logan to T. Hartley Crawford, March 3, 1845, in US Bureau of Indian Affairs, *Letters Received by the Office of Indian Affairs, 1824–81,* National Archives Microfilm Publications, microcopy M234 (Washington, DC: National Archives, 1959), reel 227.

30. "The Indian Council," *Cherokee Advocate*, May 22, 1845, [4].

31. Phineas Young, Journal, April 23–May 19, 1845, CHL.

32. Walker, "Seeking the 'Remnant,'" 18, 24.

33. Jonathan Dunham to Brigham Young, May 31, 1845, Brigham Young Office Files, CHL.

34. Phineas Young, Journal, May 19, 1845, CHL.

35. Daniel Spencer, Journal, August 3–18, 1845, CHL.

36. Council of Fifty, Minutes, September 9, 1845, in *JSP*, CFM:471.

37. Council of Fifty, Minutes, September 9, 1845, in *JSP*, CFM:472.

38. Council of Fifty, Minutes, January 11, 1846, in *JSP*, CFM:518.

Chapter 11

A MONUMENT OF THE SAINTS' INDUSTRY

The Nauvoo House and the Council of Fifty

Matthew C. Godfrey

In January 1841, Joseph Smith dictated a revelation that commanded members of the Church of Jesus Christ of Latter-day Saints to begin construction of two structures in Nauvoo, Illinois: a temple and what was designated as the Nauvoo House, a boardinghouse for travelers. At times, Joseph believed that completing the Nauvoo House was as important as finishing the temple—the spiritual center of Nauvoo—if not more so. However, delays in construction and an eventual emphasis on finishing the temple meant that the Nauvoo House was nowhere near completion at the time of Joseph's murder in June 1844. For a period of time thereafter, little was seemingly done on the house. In March 1845, however, the Council of Fifty took up the status of the Nauvoo House, and it became a periodic topic of discussion for the next several months as construction resumed. The story of these 1845 efforts has been ably told by historians using the records of the Nauvoo House Association, the journal of William Clayton, and the correspondence of George Miller, among other records.[1] However, minutes of the Council of Fifty flesh out the story, showing the role that the council played in generating support to resume construction on the building, as well as its role in supervising the efforts. The minutes demonstrate that the council had jurisdiction

This "View of Nauvoo" comes from an 1859 lithograph of a sketch by John Shroede. Detail from Map of Hancock County, Illinois (Holmes and Arnold, 1859). Courtesy of Library of Congress, Washington, DC.

over at least some of the Church's financial interests, a topic that deserves more consideration by historians.

BEGINNINGS OF THE NAUVOO HOUSE

The January 1841 revelation directed the Church to construct the Nauvoo House as a "boarding house . . . for the boarding of strangers." The structure would "be a delightful habitation for man," the revelation continued, "and a resting place for the weary traveller." George Miller, Lyman Wight, John Snider, and Peter Haws were to serve as a committee overseeing construction of the house, which would be financed from the sale of stock at fifty dollars a share. The revelation directed several individuals, including Joseph Smith, to purchase stock in the house.[2] In February 1841, the Illinois state legislature passed an act that incorporated the Nauvoo House Association, setting forth the purposes of the house and providing authorization for the issuance of stock. The act also declared that Joseph Smith "and his heirs would hold a suite of rooms in perpetual succession" in the house because it would be built on his property, something which the revelation also allowed for.[3]

Under the authority of the act and the revelation, construction on the house began in 1841, and emissaries of the Church were sent to sell stock. The building, which was originally planned as an L-shaped structure with five floors, was seen, along with the temple, as an important component of Nauvoo. Just as the Saints needed to construct the temple to show their obedience to God, they felt that they were under a divine mandate to build the Nauvoo House. Construction of the house also provided employment to many who converted to the Church in the British Isles and then emigrated to Nauvoo. Despite this labor force, and despite the importance that Joseph Smith placed on completing the structure, construction efforts were only sporadic from 1841 to 1844, in part because of work on the temple. Indeed, in March 1844, Smith asked that work on the Nauvoo House cease until the temple was completed: "We need the temple more than any thing Else."[4] By the time of Joseph's death in June 1844, only the ground floor's walls were completed.[5]

THE COUNCIL OF FIFTY AND THE NAUVOO HOUSE

In the months after Joseph Smith's death, little, if anything, was done on the house as Church members tried to cope with the loss of their leader and decide who would take his place. A few months after Brigham Young and the Twelve Apostles assumed leadership in the fall of 1844, Young resumed meetings of the Council of Fifty—an organization Joseph Smith had established in March 1844 to govern the kingdom of God on the earth. One of the questions the council examined was whether to move forward with the completion of the Nauvoo House. On March 11, 1845, the council first addressed the subject. Brigham Young, who chaired the meeting, requested "that arrangements be made forthwith to put the works in operation," but the minutes provide no further detail about these arrangements or what other considerations the council gave to the question.[6]

IMPORTANCE OF COMPLETING CONSTRUCTION

More discussion occurred at the council's March 18 meeting. Young explained that a revelation had commanded the Church to build the house, "and we have sent out men to fetch in the means to do it." Because "the stone for the Temple are about cut, and we will have a host of hands without work," Young believed it was an opportune time to resume construction on the Nauvoo House. Concerned that Church members in need of employment would abandon Nauvoo, Young proposed that they be employed on the house and that the council emphasize to the Church "that if they don't build that house they shall bear the curse of it." Young himself felt strongly about completing the work, stating that "there are sacred records deposited in the foundation of that house and it is our duty to build the house and cover up those records."[7] He proposed that shares of stock be sold at the April general conference and that George Miller, assisted by Newel K. Whitney, "call a meeting of the stockholders and enter into the work immediately."[8]

After Young spoke, other council members conveyed their support of recommencing work. Heber C. Kimball noted that three subjects occupied "his whole mind and the minds of his brethren": construction of the temple; the "western mission," whereby men were to consult with American Indian tribes about potential alliances and gathering places; and the building of the Nauvoo House. Kimball believed that the Church had sufficient means to accomplish all three of these projects, claiming that he alone could raise ten thousand dollars for them. Like Young, Kimball also supported work on the Nauvoo House because of the employment opportunities it would provide, stating that he did not want to send Church members "away among the gentiles." John Taylor believed that the Nauvoo House would make the Saints richer rather than poorer, even with monetary outlays that would need to be made. With this high level of support among the Council of Fifty, Orson Pratt moved that George Miller "settle up the books of the Nauvoo House Association, call a meeting of the Stockholders and appoint men to fill the place of the Trustees who are gone away."[9] The motion passed unanimously.[10]

SUPERVISORY ROLE

Miller, who had been serving as a trustee for the Nauvoo House since its inception, tried to carry out the council's direction. On March 22, 1845, he reported to the council that "he had taken steps to call a meeting of the Stock Holders" for April 5, but that more needed to be done to ascertain "the amount of means belonging to the Nauvoo House." One of the problems was that Lyman Wight had evidently lost a considerable number of stock certificates in 1843, leaving a question as to what certificates were actually still extant. To solve this problem, Miller proposed publishing a notice requesting that stockholders "give account of the date and numbers of the certificate[s]" that they held and that those certificates lost by Wight then be invalidated. Miller also recommended that a building plan of the house be created and that "a bill of the lumber and other materials" necessary for construction be given to the council.[11]

Miller clearly regarded the Council of Fifty as taking a supervisory role over the Nauvoo House, and other council members evidently agreed. William W. Phelps and Orson Hyde, for example, recommended the formation of a committee of council members "to investigate the affairs of the Nauvoo House." However, such a proposal—and apparently even Miller's proposals—did not sit well with Lucien Woodworth, original architect of the Nauvoo House. Woodworth declared that the committee designated in the January 1841 revelation should be the one overseeing the house. Woodworth also believed that he should play a large role in the house's construction, given that he had been appointed by the Nauvoo House committee "under the directions of president Joseph Smith to be the architect" of the building. In addition, Woodworth claimed that he had been "appointed to superintend the building of the house." Indeed, Woodworth continued, he knew as much about the house "as any committee which can be appointed."[12]

In the ensuing discussion, it became apparent that many members of the Council of Fifty were not aware of Woodworth's extensive involvement with the house. However, even after considering Woodworth's already existing role and what Miller had done and was doing on the house, council members still believed that more supervision from the Council of Fifty was necessary. A committee of Miller, Woodworth, Newel K. Whitney, William Clayton, and James Sloan (who was not a member of the council) was appointed to go through the financial papers of the Nauvoo House Association, and Woodworth was appointed to prepare a plan of the house to present to the council. Such tasks should be completed, the council voted, before the Church's April general conference.[13]

On March 25, 1845, the committee appointed by the council reported on its findings regarding the Nauvoo House Association stock, including the total number of certificates that had been issued (2,377), how many of those had been sold (348), how many were missing (272), and how many the trustees still held (1,773).[14] Because some certificates were missing, several council members advocated calling in the old stock and issuing new stock to prevent fraud, something that Peter Haws, one of the original trustees of the association, asserted Joseph Smith had told him to do. Joseph had even had new certificates printed for this purpose, Haws continued. Although there was much support among the council for this proposition, Brigham Young declared that he had spoken to Joseph Smith before his death about the issuance of new stock and that Young did not believe that it was necessary to do so "at present." Instead, he recommended that the committee's report be printed in the newspapers, including the dates of the missing certificates, thereby decreasing the chances of fraud.[15]

THE SMITH FAMILY'S INTEREST

The council also examined the question of Joseph Smith's interest in the Nauvoo House—an interest specified both in the revelation instructing the establishment of the house and in the charter of the Nauvoo House Association. Lucien Woodworth insisted that Joseph had "no claim in that house," but Brigham Young stated unequivocally that "brother Joseph and his heirs have an interest in that house." Young wanted the interest to be sold at auction, but he also declared that the Nauvoo House trustees should still deed to Joseph's heirs "the suit[e] of rooms contemplated in the house" once the building was completed. Orson Pratt then moved that the administrator of Joseph's estate—Joseph W. Coolidge, a member of the Council of Fifty—"be advised to advertise according to law the right title and interest of Joseph Smith in that house and that the Trustees for the church be advised to bid it off." The motion passed, and the April 2, 1845, issue of the *Nauvoo Neighbor* contained a notice from Coolidge that an estate sale would be held on April 12, including the sale of "all the interest of Joseph Smith deceased in the Nauvoo House Association."[16]

STOCK AND TRUSTEES

On April 5, 1845, the stockholders of the Nauvoo House Association met. Presumably because so few stockholders were in attendance, the meeting adjourned until April 7 after being called to order. On that day, several items of business were transacted, including the appointment of George A. Smith and Amasa Lyman as trustees in the association, replacing Lyman Wight and George Snider. Woodworth also displayed his plans for at least some parts of the building.[17] That afternoon, the Church met in general conference, and Young raised the subject of the Nauvoo House, asking that all those willing to purchase one share of stock in the house raise their hands. According to the minutes of the meeting, "there were so many hands uplifted that they could not possibly be counted." Young then asked for a raise of hands of those willing to purchase two shares of stock, and "quite a large number of hands were shown." When Young asked who was willing to complete the Nauvoo House, "every hand was raised in the congregation." Young then informed the group that the books of the Nauvoo House Association "would be opened in the upper part of the brick store" on April 14.[18]

On April 15, George Miller conveyed to the Council of Fifty that the association's trustees were "ready to go into active operation." He wondered whether the trustees' duties "should be investigated in this council." After some discussion, the council voted that the trustees' business should be under the supervision of the Quorum of the Twelve Apostles rather than the Council of Fifty.[19] Despite this designation, at least some business pertaining to the Nauvoo House continued to come before the council. On May 6, 1845, for example, Miller raised a question about whom deeds for property given in exchange for stock in the house be made out to. The council voted that they should be made to the trustees-in-trust of the Church.[20]

After this decision, the Nauvoo House did not appear in the minutes of the Council of Fifty again until January 1846, when Church leaders were making preparations to depart Nauvoo. At that time, Brigham Young declared that he wanted to leave a group of men in Nauvoo to "finish the Temple and perhaps the Nauvoo House, for he believes they can both be finish'd as well as not and for his part he is willing to leave all his property to finish these two houses." Later in this same meeting, Young stated that the completion of these two buildings would "stand as monuments of the industry of this people," making it important that they were completed. The council agreed, voting unanimously that both the temple and the Nauvoo House be completed. Council members also responded with a "universal no" to the question of whether the two buildings should be sold. Clearly, having been directed by revelation to complete these two buildings, Church members continued to believe it was a sacred duty to do so.[21]

CONCLUSION

The Nauvoo House was never finished. By October 1845, Willard Richards reported that the walls now approached "nearly the third story above the basement," but that may have been an exaggerated portrayal of the progress. Whatever the case, the house never came close to completion.[22] Regardless, the minutes of the Council of Fifty reemphasize what other records indicate: that construction of the building was considered a significant assignment from the Lord, akin to the establishment of the Nauvoo Temple. The minutes also provide a richer account of the role the council played in generating renewed interest in finishing the house in the spring of 1845. Had it not been for discussions in the council about the Nauvoo House, it is debatable whether the Saints would have recommenced their work. However, council members, including Brigham Young and others, considered it a sacred duty to finish the house. That deliberations about the house occurred in the Council of Fifty indicates that the council was responsible not just for examining and selecting a new gathering place for the Saints but for many of the temporal affairs of the Church. At a meeting on April 11, 1845, Young "def[ied] any man to draw the line between the spiritual and temporal affairs in the kingdom of God" and then declared that every member of the Council of Fifty "has to do with every thing between earth and heaven or hell."[23] The temporal needs of the Church were just as important as the spiritual needs, and, under Young's leadership, the council exercised its authority over temporal matters as well as spiritual ones.

NOTES

1. The most complete account of the Nauvoo House is Alex D. Smith, "Symbol of Mormonism: The Nauvoo Boarding House," *The John Whitmer Historical Association Journal* 35, no. 2 (Fall/Winter 2015): 109–36.

2. Revelation, January 19, 1841 [D&C 124], josephsmithpapers.org; Smith, "Symbol of Mormonism," 115.

3. Smith, "Symbol of Mormonism," 115–16; Revelation, January 19, 1841 [D&C 124:56], josephsmithpapers.org.

4. Joseph Smith, Journal, March 4, 1844, in Andrew H. Hedges, Alex D. Smith, and Brent M. Rogers, eds., *Journals, Volume 3: May 1843–June 1844*, vol. 3 of the Journals series of *The Joseph Smith Papers*, ed. Ronald K. Esplin and Matthew J. Grow (Salt Lake City: Church Historian's Press, 2015), 189 (hereafter *JSP*, J3); see also, Joseph Smith, Journal, March 7, 1844, in *JSP*, J3:193.

5. Smith, "Symbol of Mormonism," 117–29.

6. Council of Fifty, Minutes, March 11, 1845, in Matthew J. Grow, Ronald K. Esplin, Mark Ashurst-McGee, Gerrit J. Dirkmaat, and Jeffrey D. Mahas, eds., *Council of Fifty, Minutes, March 1844–January 1846*, vol. 1 of the Administrative Records series of *The Joseph Smith Papers*, ed. Ronald K. Esplin, Matthew J. Grow, and Matthew C. Godfrey (Salt Lake City: Church Historian's Press, 2016), 321 (hereafter *JSP*, CFM).

7. Young was referring to items placed in the cornerstone of the Nauvoo House on December 29, 1841, including the original manuscript of the Book of Mormon, Heber C. Kimball's journal, the January 1841 revelation commanding construction of the temple and the Nauvoo House, and published editions of the Book of Mormon and the Doctrine and Covenants. Joseph Smith, Journal, December 29, 1841, in Andrew H. Hedges, Alex D. Smith, and Richard Lloyd Anderson, eds., *Journals, Volume 2: December 1841–April 1843*, vol. 2 of the Journals series of *The Joseph Smith Papers*, ed. Dean C. Jessee, Ronald K. Esplin, and Richard Lyman Bushman (Salt Lake City: Church Historian's Press, 2011), 19–20.

8. Council of Fifty, Minutes, March 18, 1845, in *JSP*, CFM:344.

9. Council of Fifty, Minutes, March 18, 1845, in *JSP*, CFM:345. Those who had "gone away" were evidently Lyman Wight and John Snider. Wight had been rejected from the Council of Fifty on February 4, 1845; there is little information about Snider during this time period. Both were replaced as trustees in the Nauvoo House Association on April 7, 1845. Council of Fifty, Minutes, February 4, 1845, in *JSP*, CFM:226; Minutes, April 5–7, 1845, Nauvoo House Association Records, box 5, folder 16, CHL, MS 2375.

10. Council of Fifty, Minutes, March 18, 1845, in *JSP*, CFM:346.

11. Council of Fifty, Minutes, March 22, 1845, in *JSP*, CFM:362.

12. Council of Fifty, Minutes, March 22, 1845, in *JSP*, CFM:363.

13. Council of Fifty, Minutes, March 22, 1845, in *JSP*, CFM:364–66.

14. "Report of a Committee appointed to examine the situation of the Stock of the Nauvoo House Association," Nauvoo House Association Records, CHL.

15. Council of Fifty, Minutes, March 25, 1845, in *JSP*, CFM:381–84.

16. Council of Fifty, Minutes, March 25, 1845, in *JSP*, CFM:384–86; "Administrator's Sale," *Nauvoo Neighbor*, April 2, 1845. Although the notice was dated March 23, 1845, that may have been a mistake, given that this discussion in the Council of Fifty and its authorization of the sale did not occur until March 25.

17. Minutes, April 5–7, 1845, Nauvoo House Association Records, CHL.

18. "Conference Minutes," *Times and Seasons* 6, no. 7 (April 15, 1845): 871.

19. Council of Fifty, Minutes, April 15, 1845, in *JSP*, CFM:431.

20. Council of Fifty, Minutes, May 6, 1845, in *JSP*, CFM:442.

21. Council of Fifty, Minutes, January 11, 1846, in *JSP*, CFM:512, 519–20.

22. Willard Richards to R. C. Richards, October 15, 1845, in *Our Pioneer Heritage*, comp. Kate B. Carter (Salt Lake City: Daughters of Utah Pioneers, 1960), 3:137–38; Smith, "Symbol of Mormonism," 131n75.

23. Council of Fifty, Minutes, April 11, 1845, in *JSP*, CFM:401.

Chapter 12

"WITH FULL AUTHORITY TO BUILD UP THE KINGDOM OF GOD ON EARTH"

Lyman Wight on the Council of Fifty

Christopher James Blythe

Members of the Council of Fifty—or the kingdom of God, as it was also often called—took various positions in the succession crisis after Joseph Smith's death. The majority of council members accepted the succession claim of Brigham Young and the Twelve Apostles and in turn supported Young in 1845 as the "prophet, priest, and king" of the council.[1] On the other hand, some council members believed they had been granted special responsibilities as part of the Fifty that they could now fulfill independently of the Church's hierarchy. Others insisted that the council itself should become the governing voice of the Church.

Both Lyman Wight and Young agreed that the best course of action was to pursue the plans that Joseph Smith had revealed and prioritized before he died. Yet their zeal led these men to take starkly different roads in fulfilling these ends. This chapter examines the place of Wight in the history of the Council of Fifty, demonstrating how a man who attended only three council meetings became the council's most outspoken public advocate in the late 1840s and early 1850s. As the leader of a small colony in Texas, he spent his last years trying to live up to what he believed were his and the council's most important commissions—even when it came to him opposing his fellow members of the Quorum of Twelve Apostles.

TEXAS

Although Wight did not attend a meeting of the Council of Fifty until May 1844, his proposal for a Latter-day Saint settlement in the Republic of Texas was a major impetus for the council's preliminary meeting on March 10. Beginning in 1841, apostle Lyman Wight and bishop George Miller had been assigned to lead a colony in charge of gathering lumber in an area known as the "Pineries" in Wisconsin Territory.[2] In February 1844, Wight and other representatives from the colony wrote to Nauvoo, presenting various reasons to establish a settlement in Texas. When Joseph Smith received the letters, he appointed a committee to meet and discuss the proposal. According to Smith's journal, the committee determined to "grant their petition," including giving the "go ahead concer[n]ing the indians. & southern states &c." Apparently, the committee also discussed the possibility of sending men from the Pinery to Santa Fe to meet with Sam Houston and see if he "will embrace the gospel."[3]

Establishing a settlement in the Republic of Texas remained a central item on the Council of Fifty's 1844 agenda. On March 14, 1844, the council dispatched an emissary, Lucien Woodworth, to visit Sam Houston and discuss the possibility of a settlement.[4] Some retrospective accounts of council members went so far as to suggest that Texas was given priority in the council's discussions about colonization. For instance, George Miller recalled that the council's primary goal was "to have Joseph elected President," that thereby "the dominion of the kingdom would be forever established in the United States. And if not successful, we could but fall back on Texas, and be a kingdom notwithstanding."[5] Yet the minutes of the meetings of the Fifty reveal that Texas was only one of multiple locations considered.

On April 18, 1844, Joseph Smith even expressed his hope that Nauvoo could be recognized as an "independant government," rendering it unnecessary for the majority of the Saints to leave the region. He admitted, "I have no disposition to go to Texas, but here is Lyman Wight [who] wants to go."[6] Wight was not present for that meeting or in the council's organizational meeting when council members decided they would "look to some place where we can go and establish a Theocracy either in Texas or Oregon or somewhere in California &c."[7] In fact, when Wight arrived

Council member Lucien Woodworth traveled to the Republic of Texas in spring 1844 to negotiate with Texas president Sam Houston for a possible Mormon settlement in the republic. Daguerreotype of Houston, circa 1848 to 1850, by Mathew B. Brady studio. Courtesy of Library of Congress, Washington, DC.

in Nauvoo to be officially admitted into the council, the first meeting he attended on May 3 was dominated by discussion of Texas prompted by Woodworth's return from meeting with Houston.[8] Joseph Smith and other council members deliberated on the possibility of a future Mormon presence in the Republic of Texas, including the Saints' involvement in the struggling Texas government.

At the May 6 council meeting, Wight expressed his desire "to have those families now at the pinery go to Texas." According to the minutes, Smith agreed and "suggested the propriety of those families going to the Texas and not telling who they are." Presumably, Smith wanted to continue talks with Houston about Mormons arriving pursuant to an official agreement and thus did not want the members of the Black River Falls colony announcing their religious affiliation. Brigham Young followed Smith's remarks and moved that Wight, like other apostles, should first "go through the United States electioneering for the Presidency." Young later moved "that the brethren in the pine country be committed to the council of Ers [Elders] Wight, Woodworth and Miller." The minutes note that the proposal was "carried unanimously."[9]

This meeting held great significance for Wight throughout his life. However, when he wrote his own account of that day four years later, his version differed from the official minutes in that it emphasized Smith's role in the decisions. Wight recalled that it was Smith who brought up the Texas mission and declared, "'Let George Miller and Lyman Wight take the Black river company and their friends, and go to Texas, to the confines of Mexico, in the Cordilleras mountains; and at the same time let Brother Woodworth, who has just returned from Texas, go back to the seat of government in Texas, to intercede for a tract of country which we might have control over, that we might find a resting place for a little season.' A unanimous voice was had for both Missions." According to Wight, Smith also moved that Wight should go to the East to "'hold me up as a candidate for President of the United States at the ensuing election; and when they return let them go forth with the Black river company to perform the Mission which has been voted this day.' Which again called the unanimous voice of the Grand Council." After the meeting, Wight met with Smith in "a private chamber" where the Prophet spoke further about the Texas mission and told him that if Congress rejected a proposal for the Saints to raise troops to defend Texas, "'get 500,000 if you can and go into that country.' He instructed me faithfully concerning the above Mission."[10]

WIGHT'S COMMISSION TO TEXAS

Not surprisingly, when Wight returned to Nauvoo from his electioneering mission after Joseph Smith's martyrdom, he was eager to begin this commission. On August 12, 1844, during a meeting of the Quorum of the Twelve, Wight expressed his desire to take the Black River Falls colony to Texas. The apostles, perhaps grudgingly, passed a resolution "that Lyman Wight go to Texas as he chooses, with his company, also George Miller and Lucien Woodworth, and carry out the instructions he has received from Joseph—to procure a location."[11] This was far from a breaking point between Wight and Young, but it was the beginning of Wight's estrangement from the Church.

Young warned Wight that he did not want others outside of the Black River Falls company accompanying him to Texas. His concern seems to have been that Wight would draw off resources—both human and material—from Nauvoo, which would render the construction of the temple and a future exodus, if necessary, much more difficult. He even cautioned Wight that he "would have to speak a little against [his] going for fear the whole Church to a man would turn out."[12] Wight agreed to this condition. Likewise, when Heber C. Kimball urged the colony that had relocated to Nauvoo in July to first move to Wisconsin before making the trek to Texas, Wight complied.[13] In these early days after the martyrdom, Wight seems to have seen himself as completely loyal to his fellow apostles. He supported the Twelve's taking the lead of the Church, which he viewed as a strategic move to withstand "aspiring men," such as Sidney Rigdon and James Strang, who were seeking to be recognized as prophets over the Church.[14] On November 6, 1844, the colony in Wisconsin publicly sustained "the Twelve Apostles of this church in their state and standing and all other authorities with them."[15]

RUPTURE WITH THE QUORUM OF THE TWELVE

On the other hand, observable fractures in the relationship between Wight and the Twelve seemed evident during the October 1844 conference in Nauvoo. The minutes, as published in the *Times and Seasons* the following month, stated that Brigham Young referred to "Wight's going away because he was a coward."[16] While Young may have been simply fulfilling his promise to Wight that he would "speak a little against" the mission, Wight was greatly offended by the barb.[17] Sentiment toward Wight in Nauvoo was changing. Rumors were circulating that Wight was not actually as loyal to the Twelve as he pretended.[18] In February 1845, when Young revived the Council of Fifty, Wight with several others was expelled from the kingdom.[19] In April, the Twelve sent a messenger to Wight's colony—who had already begun their trek to Texas—with a letter, counseling them to abandon their plans to go west until after they could receive their endowments in the temple.[20] Directly disobeying orders for what seems to have been the first time, Wight continued to lead his colony on their southwestern journey. The colony eventually settled near Austin in a village they named Zodiac.[21] During the October 1845 conference, Church leaders deliberated on whether he should remain a member of the Quorum of the Twelve.[22]

From Texas, Wight may have become increasingly aware of the Church's diminishing opinion of him and the Texas mission from the *Times and Seasons* or occasional visitors, but it was the arrival of George Miller that set him off. Miller, who had remained in Nauvoo, joined the Texas colony in 1848 after his own falling out with Brigham Young. He likely brought word that Wight had been expelled from the Council of Fifty in February 1845, when Young had revived the kingdom.[23] It was shortly after Miller's arrival that Wight, now incensed, decided to publicly defend his position and standing in the Church. The result was a sixteen-page pamphlet titled *An Address by the Way of an Abridged Account and Journal of My Life from February 1844 up to April 1848, with an Appeal to the Latter-day Saints.*

The first nine pages followed Wight's life from his proposal for a Mormon colony in Texas to his eventual journey to Texas by way of

Wisconsin, touching on his initiation into the Council of Fifty, electioneering mission, and return to Nauvoo. This is a noteworthy publication because of Wight's candidness about the details of the Council of Fifty. Likely because members of the Fifty swore an oath of secrecy on admission to the council, there are no comparable public histories of the Fifty. Wight's willingness to ignore this vow is unusual, but he may have believed this was his only means to defend his position. He characterized the Fifty as an ecclesiastical organization. It was the "Grand Council of the Church, or in other words, the perfect organization of the Church of Jesus Christ of Latter Day Saints on earth. This council consisted of fifty members, with full authority to build up the Kingdom of God on earth, that his will might be done on earth as in heaven."[24] He also explained, as noted above, his specific assignment to begin a settlement in Texas.

In the second half of the pamphlet—what Wight termed his "appeal"—he defended his character and his place as one of the Twelve Apostles, and protested his removal from the Council of Fifty. He explicitly challenged "those of a like ordination unto myself that they have neither power nor authority given them, to move me from this station, nor to place any long eared Jack Ass to fill a place, which has never been vacated. . . . I have not forfeited my right, title nor claim to a seat with the Twelve, neither with the Grand Council of God on the earth."[25] Finally, he invited "all ye inhabitants of the earth" to join him on his mission in Texas.[26]

Ultimately, the pamphlet was the point of no return for Wight's relationship with the Church as continued under the authority of the Quorum of Twelve Apostles. He sent messengers to distribute the pamphlet to Latter-day Saint branches in Iowa and throughout the Midwest.[27] Just as Wight had prioritized his commission to establish a settlement in Texas over the apostles' efforts to construct the temple in Nauvoo, his pamphlet clarified that he viewed other colonization efforts as inferior to his own. More important, what the pamphlet revealed was that the division between Brigham Young and Lyman Wight had less to do with their competing priorities than it did with their fundamental interpretations of the Council of Fifty. Young saw the Council of

Fifty as an nonecclesiastical institution organized for deliberating on political concerns. He viewed the council as an important fulfillment of prophecy, but he also believed it was subservient to the needs of the Church and was rightfully under the direction of the Church's leadership. Wight saw the Council of Fifty as the highest ecclesiastical institution of the Church. For Wight, the Twelve should report to the Fifty and not the other way around.

DIFFERING OPINIONS ON THE ROLE OF THE FIFTY

Wight was not the only council member to have held the belief that the Fifty was a new governing body over the Church. On April 18, 1844, the council devoted much of an afternoon meeting to resolving differing opinions on whether "the kingdom of God and the church of God are one and the same thing" or whether "the church is one thing and the kingdom another." Joseph Smith concluded this discussion by explaining that "there is a distinction between the Church of God and kingdom of God. . . . The church is a spiritual matter and a spiritual kingdom; but the kingdom which Daniel saw was not a spiritual kingdom, but was designed to be got up for the safety and salvation of the saints by protecting them in their religious rights and worship."[28] While this resolved the debate during Smith's lifetime, only a month after the martyrdom, two members of the Council of Fifty wanted to "call together the Council of Fifty and organize the church." Church leaders rebuffed the idea and explained "that the organization of the church belonged to the Priesthood alone."[29] James Emmett, like Wight, also set out on a mission based on a commission he received from the Council of Fifty. His company spoke of the Council of Fifty as "the highest court on earth."[30]

Yet, by 1848, there were few advocates for this interpretation that the Council of Fifty should govern the Church. Wight's pamphlet seems to have revived this sentiment among at least some members of the council. Council members Lucien Woodworth and Peter Haws visited Zodiac, perhaps with intentions to stay.[31] As council member Alpheus Cutler started his own mission with connections to the Fifty, his followers likewise met with Wight.[32] In 1853, Cutler established a church with himself as the head, arguing that the original Church had gone into apostasy but that he possessed higher authority as a member of the kingdom. While we cannot be certain what degree Wight's pamphlet influenced Cutler's position that the kingdom was superior to the Church, it is an interesting coincidence that there would be a dialogue between these communities at that time.[33] Peter Haws, on the other hand, was inspired to defend Wight's position to Church leaders in Iowa. After his return from Texas, Haws demanded Orson Hyde "call together the Council of Fifty, as there was important buisness to be attended to, and it was necessary that, that body should meet immediately as there was feelings, and important buisness to attend to."[34] Memorably, he accused Brigham Young of failing "to carry out the measures of Joseph" by not fully utilizing the Council of Fifty, declaring "the Twelve had swallowed up thirty eight."[35] That is, the Twelve had usurped the responsibility and authority that Smith had intended for the Fifty.

CONCLUSION

As Lyman Wight and his settlement in Texas had fewer interactions with other Latter-day Saint communities, the Council of Fifty still remained crucial to Zodiac's identity. Local branch meetings even went so far as to publicly recognize "Lyman and George [Miller] in their standing as two of the Fifties."[36] Wight continued to reflect on what the Fifty should have done after the martyrdom. In 1851, he wrote that "the fifties assembled should have called on all the authorities of the church down to the lay-members from all the face of the earth" and sustained the leadership of Joseph Smith III, who would have taken the lead of completing the temple. "Then," Wight continued, "should the fifty have sallied forth unto all the world, and built up according to the pattern which Bro. Joseph had given; the Twelve to have acted in two capacities, one in opening the gospel in all the world, and organizing churches; and then what would have been still greater, to have counseled in the Grand Council of heaven, in gathering in the house of Israel and establishing Zion to be thrown down no more forever."[37] In 1853, Wight still maintained his hope that "the majority of the fifty, which Br. Joseph organized, [would] assume their place and standing."[38]

NOTES

1. Council of Fifty, Minutes, March 1, 1845, in Matthew J. Grow, Ronald K. Esplin, Mark Ashurst-McGee, Gerrit J. Dirkmaat, and Jeffrey D. Mahas, eds., *Council of Fifty, Minutes, March 1844–January 1846*, vol. 1 of the Administrative Records series of *The Joseph Smith Papers*, ed. Ronald K. Esplin, Matthew J. Grow, and Matthew C. Godfrey (Salt Lake City: Church Historian's Press, 2016), 256 (hereafter *JSP*, CFM).

2. See Matthew J. Grow and Brian Whitney, "The Pinery Saints: Mormon Communalism at Black River Falls, Wisconsin," *Communal Societies* 36, no. 2 (2016): 153–70.

3. Joseph Smith, Journal, March 10, 1844, in Andrew H. Hedges, Alex D. Smith, and Brent M. Rogers, eds., *Journals, Volume 3: May 1843–June 1844*, vol. 3 of the Journals series of *The Joseph Smith Papers*, ed. Ronald K. Esplin and Matthew J. Grow (Salt Lake City: Church Historian's Press, 2015), 201 (hereafter *JSP*, J3).

4. Joseph Smith, Journal, March 14, 1844, in *JSP*, J3:204.

5. George Miller, Letter to "Dear Brother," June 28, 1855, *Northern Islander*, September 6, 1855.

6. Council of Fifty, Minutes, April 18, 1844, in *JSP*, CFM: 127–28.

7. Council of Fifty, Minutes, March 11, 1844, in *JSP*, CFM:40.

8. Council of Fifty, Minutes, May 3, 1844, in *JSP*, CFM:137–47.

9. Council of Fifty, Minutes, May 6, 1844, in *JSP*, CFM:157–58.

10. Lyman Wight, *An Address by the Way of an Abridged Account and Journal of My Life from February 1844 up to April 1848, with an Appeal to the Latter-day Saints* (1848), 3–4. The actual petition was not limited to Texas, but included Oregon as well. See Council of Fifty, Minutes, March 26, 1844, in *JSP*, CFM:67–70.

11. Willard Richards, Journal, August 12, 1844, Church History Library, Salt Lake City.

12. Lyman Wight, Letter to Brigham Young, March 2, 1857, Church History Library.

13. Heber C. Kimball, Journal, August 23, 1844, in Stanley B. Kimball, ed., *On the Potter's Wheel: The Diaries of Heber C. Kimball* (Salt Lake City: Signature Books, 1987), 82.

14. Wight, Letter to "Dear Brother and Sister," November 29, 1844, in Wight, *An Address*, 5.

15. Crawford County Branch (Wisconsin), Minutes, November 6, 1844, Church History Library.

16. "Conference Minutes," *Times and Seasons*, November 1, 1844, 5:694.

17. Lyman Wight to Brigham Young, March 2, 1857, Church History Library.

18. William Clayton, Journal, September 25, 1844, in George D. Smith, ed., *An Intimate Chronicle: The Journals of William Clayton* (Salt Lake City: Signature Books, 1991), 545.

19. Council of Fifty, Minutes, February 4, 1845, in *JSP*, CFM:226.

20. See Quorum of Twelve to Lyman Wight "and all the brethren with him," April 17, 1845, Brigham Young Collection, Church History Library.

21. See Melvin C. Johnson, *Polygamy on the Pedernales: Lyman Wight's Mormon Villages in Antebellum Texas, 1845 to 1858* (Logan: Utah State University, 2006), chaps. 3–4.

22. "Conference Minutes," *Times and Seasons*, November 1, 1845, 6:1009.

23. Council of Fifty, Minutes, February 4, 1845, in *JSP*, CFM:226.

24. Wight, *An Address*, 3.

25. Wight, *An Address*, 12.

26. Wight, *An Address*, 16.

27. Lucius Scovil to Samuel Brannan, December 17, 1848, Church History Library.

28. Council of Fifty, Minutes, April 18, 1844, in *JSP*, CFM:121, 128.

29. History, 1838–1856, vol. F-1, Addenda, 9, Church History Library.

30. William D. Kartchner, Reminiscences and Diary, 19, Church History Library. For a discussion of Emmett's mission, see Jeffrey D. Mahas, "'The Lamanites Will Be Our Friends': Mormon Eschatology and the Development of a Mormon-Indian Racial Identity in the Council of Fifty," unpublished.

31. Lucius Scovill to Samuel Brannan, December 17, 1848, Church History Library.

32. See Danny Jorgensen, "Conflict in the Camps of Israel: The 1853 Cutlerite Schism," *Journal of Mormon History* 21 (Spring 1995): 41–42.

33. For Cutler's understanding of the Council of Fifty, see Christopher James Blythe, "The Church and the Kingdom of God: Ecclesiastical Interpretations of the Council of Fifty," *Journal of Mormon History* 43, no. 2 (2017): 113–16.

34. Orson Hyde, George A. Smith, and Ezra T. Benson, Report to "Presidents Brigham Young, Heber C Kimball, Willard Richards, and the Authorities of the Church of Jesus Christ of Latter Day Saints in Zion," April 5, 1849, Church History Library.

35. Hyde et al., Report, April 5, 1849.

36. William Leyland, Sketches on the Life and Travels of William Leyland, Community of Christ Library and Archives, Independence, Missouri, 20.

37. This document was quoted in *The History of the Reorganized Church of Jesus Christ of Latter Day Saints* (Independence, MO: Herald House, 1896), 2:791. The original was destroyed in the Herald Publishing House fire in 1907.

38. Lyman Wight, Letter to Benjamin Wight, January 1853, Community of Christ Library and Archives.

Chapter 13

"WE ARE A KINGDOM TO OURSELVES"

The Council of Fifty Minutes and the Mormon Exodus West

Richard E. Bennett

In June 2016 at the annual Mormon History Association conference, I participated on a panel discussion concerning the about-to-be-released Council of Fifty minutes. This remarkable resource has since been published and now forms part of the Administrative Records series of the Joseph Smith Papers Project. My comments at that time centered on how these minutes shed new light on a variety of topics. These topics included the political role of the Council of Fifty, the plans to unite with and convert the various tribes of Indians in the American West, the so-called "Western Mission," the building of the Nauvoo Temple and more especially the Nauvoo House, and the Saints' ultimate destination in the Rocky Mountains. I noted that in the minutes there was a definite shift in tone between the topics, designs, and purposes of this previously secret council during Joseph Smith's lifetime and those covered during Brigham Young's role as chairman. Under Joseph Smith, there was a good deal of talk about government, constitutions, and policies; under Brigham Young, the council had much more concrete discussion of plans and preparations for the pending exodus. After Joseph's martyrdom and particularly following the revocation of the Nauvoo charter in January 1845, these minutes take on an air of greater urgency as the council engaged in more studious preparation than before. No doubt this hastening was in light of growing persecution and the realization that the Latter-day Saints would have to vacate Nauvoo sooner than later and perhaps begin their exodus west as early as February 1, 1846. The purpose of this paper is to probe more deeply into the role that the Council of Fifty played in the planning and preparation for the exodus.

GENERAL PARAMETERS OF THE DESTINATION

As a student of the Mormon migrations west, I have long been of the opinion that when the Saints began leaving Nauvoo, Brigham Young and the Twelve Apostles, at that time the united leadership of the Church, did not have a precise destination in mind. They knew they were looking at the Rocky Mountains and possibly some good valley therein as possibilities, but their destination became clearer the further west they traveled.[1] While this is still partially true, the Council of Fifty minutes shed new light on the exodus, the preparations for it, the challenges the Saints would face, and what Church leaders were looking for in a new home. I discuss these topics below but especially how leaders zeroed in on the Great Salt Lake Valley as their primary destination, at least as a vantage point for later, more careful explorations of surrounding areas. Concluded Brigham Young in late 1845, "We have designed sending them somewhere near the Great Salt Lake and after we get there, in a little time we can work our way to the head of the California Bay."[2]

The minutes shed more light on *what* they were looking for in a destination than precisely *where* they were heading. The size of the place they would settle in was a major factor in their thinking—it needed to be quite large. On behalf of the entire council, Orson Spencer wrote that the Saints were "willing to accept of any eligible location within any part of the Territory of the U. States" so long as it was large enough to accommodate at least 500,000 people. "A portion of Territory not less than 200 miles square would be none too great or roomy for the increase of the people arising in a period of 10 years judging from the analogy of 10 years that have gone by."[3] Such a statement reflects leaders' combined optimism, largely borne out of the impressive success of the Twelve in their mission to Great Britain from 1838 to 1841, that the Church was destined for spectacular growth and that Nauvoo could never accommodate such swelling ranks of membership in the best of times. Seen in their deliberations was an optimism that missionary work was going to become ever more successful and that, in short order, hundreds of thousands of people would be converted and emigrate to wherever the headquarters of the Church would be located. In reality, it would take at least sixty years to meet this threshold. Thus, the members of the Council of Fifty may have been overly optimistic in their rosy projections of Church growth, but they were thinking big—very big—and envisioned a new location, a new "kingdom" as some members of the council called it, that must accommodate such favorable anticipations.

SPACE FOR AMERICAN INDIAN ALLIES

This anticipated imminent spike in membership may also be attributed to their robust expectation of not merely making allies with the various Indian tribes in the West, but also of converting them in large numbers. Said chairman Brigham Young, "The object of this organization [the Council of Fifty] is to find a place where we can dwell in peace and lift up the standard of liberty. It is for the purpose of uniting the Lamanites, and sowing the seeds of the gospel among them. They will receive it en Masse."[4] The council firmly believed that the Lamanites were modern Israel and that the martyrdom signaled the definite end of the day of the Gentiles. The Lord's Spirit was therefore about to effect a bounteous harvest of conversion upon the American Indians, fellow exiles in the West since at least Andrew Jackson's Indian Removal Act of 1830. Any movement west would of necessity bring the Saints into contact with many of these wounded and disenfranchised tribes and provide ample opportunities for preaching the gospel to them. Some members of the council therefore believed the exodus would result not only in finding a new place of settlement but also in a rich harvest of thousands of converted Native American peoples. Again, this proved an overly naive and optimistic prediction, and one that was somewhat characteristic of the unrealistic tone of much of the council's deliberations.

There was more, however, to the Indian question than conversion. The minutes are replete with references to the possibility of the Saints aligning themselves with the tribes not merely to defend themselves but to wreak vengeance upon the nation that had so viciously turned upon them. Some on the council envisioned the tribes being instrumental in helping the Saints return to their New Jerusalem (Zion) in Independence, Missouri:

"We are Legislators, set here to legislate for the best means whereby the chosen seed shall return that they might go to Jerusalem and receive the statutes they once rejected. Zion is the place where the tribes shall return and bring a present to the Lord of Hosts."[5] Council member George Miller, a well-known scout of the Iowa Territory who knew many of the tribal leaders personally, believed that the leading object of their pending mission was "to unite the tribes from North to South," for they "are ready to come forth and take hold of the matter in earnest." He continued at another meeting, "Our object is to unite all the Indian tribes from north to south and west to the Pacific Ocean in one body and to include ourselves in the number. . . . This nation has severed us from them and we are a kingdom to ourselves; and if the crisis come we can make honorable reprisals, and have enough to carry us to the farthest corner of the earth. . . . He is in favor of immediate action, and don't want to see the ship rot on the stocks, let us la[u]nch her and go to work in earnest." Having formed these Native alliances, Brigham Young stated, the Saints will "come back and sweep Jackson County and build the Temple."[6]

These kind of exaggerated, sometimes vitriolic statements lend credence to the "Lamanism" of Alpheus Cutler, who broke with the Church at Winter Quarters in 1848 in large measure because of what he felt was Brigham Young's denunciation of the Indian plan of alliance. Cutler preached this doctrine of "Lamanism" openly on the east side of the Missouri River.[7]

The fact that Young later dismissed some of his own earlier predictions, let alone the talk of some other members of the council, underscores the need to read these minutes with caution. The council deliberated courses of action. It did not dictate them, and few binding resolutions were made. Members gave advice and insights, but they did not ultimately determine action. It was essentially a deliberative body of "legislators" and advisers that expressed all kinds of different and often contrasting opinions, with some members far more vocal—and hawkish—than others. This matter of Indian conversion is a case in point. By late 1847, Brigham Young had realized that mass Native American conversions were not happening and that their once-discussed alliance with the Indian tribes was an impossibility. To talk of such things at Winter Quarters was tantamount to declaring war upon the United States and upon the state of Missouri. Thus what was said in the privacy of Council of Fifty meetings and what was decided upon during the exodus itself as the Saints moved west, were not always the same. Unlike the Quorum of the Twelve, the Council of Fifty did not exist as a separate governing body over the Church, although it is apparent that some apparently wished it would be.

DEFENSIBLE BORDERS
AND A HEALTHY CLIMATE

Another consideration in selecting their destination was that it should be a place of safety whence they could not easily be dislodged. The Mormons had learned bitter lessons from their expulsions from both Jackson and Caldwell Counties in Missouri and now from Illinois, and it was uppermost in their minds that wherever they went, it be almost impregnable and unassailable militarily from without. Said Charles C. Rich, later apostle to Bear River country, "All we want is a place to gather the women and children and when they are safe there will be no difficulty in defending ourselves as we might see proper."[8] Almon W. Babbitt, Esq., added, "It is wisdom to seek out a place with natural fortifications, where we can naturally defend ourselves."[9] The conversion of thousands of Indians would bring greater safety still: "We would be glad to have the Indians put in possession of the arms," and "when the blow is to be struck, and our object is accomplished in effecting the union, the enemy will be scattered."[10]

Of equal importance in evaluating possible destinations was the matter of the Saints' health and well-being. Nauvoo had proven to be a sickly place, especially in its formative years. Despite all the fanfare of it being the "city beautiful," Joseph Smith once described it as "a deathly sickly hole" and while painting as bright a picture as possible in order to attract emigrants, admitted that "we have been keeping up appearances, and holding out inducements, to encourage emigration that we scarcely think justifiable in consequence of the mortality that almost invariably awaits those who come from far distant parts."[11] The truth is, the Latter-day Saints lost more lives to disease than to persecution! "If we can find a healthy country we will go there," Brigham Young said.[12]

DECIDING ON A DESTINATION

With these and other considerations in mind, what place would best fill the Saints' needs? A close look at the minutes indicates a progression of thinking, a gradual refinement in plans. It would appear that in the spring of 1845, Church leaders had more or less agreed upon Upper California. At that time, California was part of the expansive northern territory of Mexico sprawling all over much of the western part of today's United States, loosely governed and poorly understood. But to the Saints, it meant a place south of Oregon and likely on the coast. John Taylor even composed the favorite song of the council, titled "The Upper California" (sung to the tune of "The Rose That All Are Praising"), in celebration of the likelihood of their going there. Sung on numerous occasions and even later in the temple, its fourth verse was as follows:

> We'll reign, we'll rule, & triumph & God shall be our king
> The plains, the hills & vallies, shall with Hosannas ring
> Our towers and temples there shall rise
> *Along the great Pacific Sea.*
> In upper California, O thats the land for me.[13]

The advantages of settling on the coast were many. Said Brigham Young, "Our final object is to get on the sea coast where we can have the advantages of commercial navigation."[14] The coast would be more fertile than inland, the climate more agreeable, and it would certainly be more conducive to emigration and to pursuing worldwide missionary work. John Taylor frowned on the idea of settling in the "barren deserts" of the interior. By building their city on the coasts, they could "carry the gospel to the other parts of the globe" more easily and efficiently.[15] Erastus Snow agreed, "If we pitch upon California, and that seems to be the place where our feelings centre, we can take care of ourselves. He often heard the prophet speak of that country last spring. He was always opposed to the idea of seeking a location in the interior where we should be cut off from the advantages of communication by the seas."[16]

But by late summer of 1845, sentiments had certainly changed, with the council now favoring an interior valley destination, something they called "the Oregon expedition," likely in an effort to disguise their true intent. The reasons for the change are not easy to decipher. Orson Hyde, never a proponent of leaving the United States in the first place, believed an interior valley within the United States to be their best option. "We could then make our own laws for our own [territorial] government and would be shielded by the constitution of the United States. . . . Should we go to California there is the same blood runs there as here and the same feelings of opposition to the truth would soon manifest themselves. We will find mobocrats there."[17]

Besides isolation, distance was also a factor. Why travel 2,100 miles if 1,500 miles would do? An obvious factor leaders considered was the preparation of their own families, wives, and children at a time of increasing persecution. Could the Latter-day Saints as a people make such an extended journey all the way to the coast?

Another pivotal consideration was the matter of Mormon livestock. The Mormons may have been money poor, but they were cattle rich. There would be tens of thousands of head of cattle in the pending exodus. Cornelius Lott, a member of the council and an excellent herdsman, was later put in charge of the Mormon livestock and played a critical role in the movement west of somewhere between ten thousand and thirty thousand head of cattle.[18] The requirement to move so many cows, oxen, sheep, chickens, horses, and other farm animals influenced leaders' choice of routes and distances. Driving that many animals up and over the mountains would be a formidable task. The difference between the Great Salt Lake and the coast, for instance, was at least six hundred more miles of additional herding, no small consideration.

Another factor was undoubtedly the publication of John C. Frémont's report of his 1842 expedition to the Rocky Mountains and his 1843–44 exploration of Upper California and Oregon, which included surveying the area around the Great Salt Lake. This study, titled *Report of the Exploring Expedition to the Rocky Mountains in the Year 1842, and to Oregon and North California in the Years 1843–'44,* was published in August 1845, but Orson Hyde had obtained an earlier version of it (reporting on only the 1842 expedition) as early as April 1844. "Judge [Stephen A.] D[ouglas] borrowed it of Mr. [Thomas Hart] B[enton] [Frémont's father-in-law]. I was not to tell any one in this city [where] I got it. The book is a most valuable document to any one contemplating a journey to Oregon."[19] The *Nauvoo Neighbor* later recorded that "the Rocky Mountains are shown to

REPORT

OF

THE EXPLORING EXPEDITION

TO

THE ROCKY MOUNTAINS

IN THE YEAR 1842,

AND

TO OREGON AND NORTH CALIFORNIA

IN THE YEARS 1843-'44.

BY

BREVET CAPT. J. C. FRÉMONT,

OF THE TOPOGRAPHICAL ENGINEERS,

UNDER THE ORDERS OF COL. J. J. ABERT, CHIEF OF THE TOPOGRAPHICAL BUREAU.

————————

PRINTED BY ORDER OF THE HOUSE OF REPRESENTATIVES.

————————

WASHINGTON:

BLAIR AND RIVES, PRINTERS.

1845.

Title page of John C. Frémont's 1845 report. Courtesy of Church History Library.

be not the formidable barriers supposed. Capt. Fremont crossed them at four different places—instead of being desolate and impassable they are shown to have many excellent passes, of which the South pass is the finest, and to embosom beautiful valleys, rivers, and parks, with lakes and

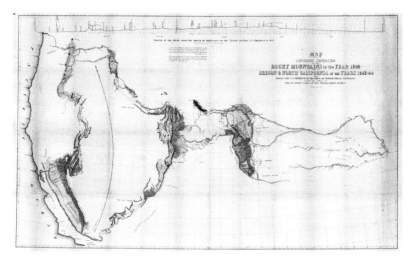

In evaluating possible destinations for a new Mormon settlement, Church leaders studied John C. Frémont's reports of his western expeditions. This map was published in John C. Frémont, *Report of the Exploring Expedition to the Rocky Mountains in the Year 1842, and to Oregon and North California in the Years 1843–'44* (Washington, DC: Blair and Rives, 1845). Courtesy of Church History Library, Salt Lake City.

mineral springs, rivalling and surpassing the most enchanting parts of the Alpine regions in Switzerland."[20] Thus the Saints were studying Frémont's maps at least a year and a half before their departure.

ANNOUNCEMENT OF PLANS

With all these considerations in mind, Brigham Young announced in one of the last meetings of the Council of Fifty in September 1845, "It has been proved that there is not much difficulty in sending people beyond the mountains. We have designed sending them somewhere near the Great Salt Lake and after we get there, in a little time we can work our way to the head of the California Bay, or the Bay of the St Francisco."[21] Added Parley P. Pratt:

> There is a good Wagon Road to California leading on from Independance Missouri. It follows the Platte, going in between the mountains, after which the roads fork, one going to California and the other to Oregon. At the place where the roads fork is the spot

where we have some notion of settling. The rout to San Francisco . . . would be about 2100 miles, but to the place where we calculate to go not more than 1500.[22]

And in one of the council meetings held within a month of the departure of the first companies, Brigham Young said that their destination would be best located somewhere out of the United States but east of the coast, if not a permanent site then certainly one from which they could scout out other possibilities. "[My] mind is to go just beyond the Rocky mountains," he said on January 11, 1846,

> somewhere on the Mexican claim and the United States will have no
> business to come there and if they do we will treat them as enemies.
> We can make a stand somewhere on the vallies of the Bear River. . . .
> Whenever we get ourselves planted in that region of country we can
> send scouts to explore the whole country to the coast and seek out
> suitable places where we can locate and fortify ourselves so as to bid
> defiance to the enemy; and also where the Saints from the Eastern
> States and England could land and establish themselves.[23]

And as to their intended route, they had long concluded the following: "In case of a removal . . . , Nauvoo is the place of general rendezvous," said Orson Hyde.

> Our course from thence would be westward through Iowa, bearing
> a little north, untill we come to the Missouri river, leaving the State
> of Missouri on the left, thence onward till we come to the Platte,
> thence up the north fork of the Platte to the mouth of [the] Sweet
> water River in Long. 107"45" W. and thence up said Sweet water
> river to the South pass of the Rocky Mountains about 11 hundred
> miles from Nauvoo, And from said South pass Lat 42° 28" north to
> the Umqua and Clamet valleys in Oregon bordering on California.[24]

As to the time of their departure, the so-called "committee on foreign relations," established back on March 4, 1845, and chaired by Samuel Bent, was initially charged with the planning and outfitting of the "Western Mission" or western expedition.[25] But as the time of the exodus drew near, the entire

Council of Fifty assumed responsibility for organizing their wholesale departure. While a concrete departure date was not mentioned for several months,
as early as September 1845 they were thinking of a spring 1846 departure. By
the beginning of 1846, there was talk of little else, even if it meant leaving in
winter, which surprisingly held out certain benefits. "If there is an advance
company to go and put in crops this spring," said Orson Pratt in January, "it
will be necessary to start by the first of February for we cannot cross the
mountains to Bear River in less than three months and we could not get there
soon enough to put in spring crops unless we start quickley." John Taylor
echoed Pratt's sentiments: "He approves of an early start. If we start in one
month while the ground is hard and froze we could take extra grain, nearly
enough to sustain our teams all the way." Phelps agreed: "If we can transplant
this kingdom while the ground is frozen we shall accomplish a great thing."[26]

And as to the makeup of the advance companies, Brigham Young said
that the company captains should "use their influence to have as few women
and children as possible, go with the first company, but let us go and prepare
a place for them, so that they can follow in the spring." "The next thing is for
every man of this council to select his fifty men who can be prepared to start
immediately either night or day when the word is given." Fearing possible government intervention, Young said, "The government of the United States have
laid plans to take the Twelve and some others of this council, and they calculate
to send a regiment of troops to take them but we can go as fast as they can."[27]

And so the time grew near, and the era of preparation was almost over.
The spirit of departure permeated the penultimate meeting of the council,
as evidenced by the following:

> We want to go whether we are ready or not. "The Lord is going to
> find this nation something to do, besides hunt after the blood of the
> saints and innocent men. . . ."
> He then called for the reports of the Captains of companies. . . .

Of the 25 companies of 100 families each now organizing, 20 companies
by their captains made report, the sum total of said reports are as follows:

> 916 Horses, 639 Wagons, 18 Buggs [buggies], 227 Yoke of Oxen
> 251 Cows, 54 men and Guns, and 70 teams ready to start at one
> hours notice.[28]

CONCLUSION

In summary, I wish to emphasize three things that have impressed me as I have more carefully studied these minutes. The first is that the Council of Fifty was not a legislative or Church administrative body. Although the council did pass resolutions, they seemed not to have been binding, nor did the council determine ultimate Church policy. Likewise, the Council of Fifty did not attempt to define Church doctrines and beliefs. Deliberative in nature, it primarily gave counsel and advice.

A second contribution is that the minutes provide a glimpse into the character of Brigham Young, who would shortly be leading the exodus. When he became chairman of the council, he directed it not in a dictating or controlling manner, but in a way that invited participation. Everyone had a voice and expressed himself freely, doing so in an advisory capacity. Brigham Young was growing into his leadership roles, and any future biography of this great Mormon leader must take these minutes into serious consideration.

Finally, the minutes of the Council of Fifty are an important help to the study of the Mormon exodus. While they corroborate much of the best current research on the exodus, they nevertheless add valuable insights and perspectives. More was said about what they were looking for in a future destination than precisely where they were going. The spaciousness of their future Zion, health concerns, safety, and the role of the American Indians—these were their earlier considerations. But as time went by, and especially after the martyrdom of Joseph Smith, there developed a tone of urgency and greater clarity in regard to their final destination, the organization of their departing companies, the concerns over their livestock, their intended route, their preparations, and the timing of their departure.

NOTES

1. "The fact remains that if he ever did anticipate it, Brigham Young referred to it in only vague, obscure generalities without ever specifying a timetable or particular place of settlement." Richard E. Bennett, *Mormons at the Missouri, 1846–1852: "And Should We Die . . ."* (Norman: University of Oklahoma Press, 1987), 16.

2. Council of Fifty, Minutes, September 9, 1845, in Matthew J. Grow, Ronald K. Esplin, Mark Ashurst-McGee, Gerrit J. Dirkmaat, and Jeffrey D. Mahas, eds., *Council of Fifty, Minutes, March 1844–January 1846*, vol. 1 of the Administrative Records series of *The Joseph Smith Papers*, ed. Ronald K. Esplin, Matthew J. Grow, and Matthew C. Godfrey (Salt Lake City: Church Historian's Press, 2016), 472 (hereafter *JSP*, CFM).

3. Council of Fifty, Minutes, February 4, 1845, in *JSP*, CFM:243.

4. Council of Fifty, Minutes, March 1, 1845, in *JSP*, CFM:255.

5. William W. Phelps, in Council of Fifty, Minutes, March 4, 1845, in *JSP*, CFM:286.

6. Council of Fifty, Minutes, March 4 and 22, 1845, in *JSP*, CFM:289, 355–56. Said Reynolds Cahoon, "It is a part of this mission to go from tribe to tribe and feel after their wise men and ordain presidents & set their own wise men up as councillors. . . . And if the enemies do not let us alone we will call out these men of the forest and they had better let us alone." Council of Fifty Minutes, March 4, 1845, in *JSP*, CFM:284.

7. See the author's article "Lamanism, Lymanism, and Corn Fields," *Journal of Mormon History* 13 (1986–87): 44–59.

8. Council of Fifty, Minutes, March 22, 1845, in *JSP*, CFM:353.

9. Council of Fifty, Minutes, March 11, 1845, in *JSP*, CFM:307.

10. Charles C. Rich and Orson Hyde, in Council of Fifty, Minutes, April 11, 1845, in *JSP*, CFM:408.

11. Joseph Smith to Horace Hotchkiss, August 25, 1841, josephsmithpapers.org. The mortality rate in Nauvoo in 1840 was thirty deaths per one thousand people. Evan Ivie and Douglas C. Heiner, "Deaths in Early Nauvoo, Illinois, 1839–1846, and in Winter Quarters, Nebraska, 1846–1848," *Religious Educator* 10, no. 3 (2009): 163–74.

12. Council of Fifty, Minutes, March 11, 1845, in *JSP*, CFM:309.

13. Council of Fifty, Minutes, April 11, 1845, in *JSP*, CFM:402, emphasis added. The song was later included in Latter-day Saint hymnals. Peter Crawley, *A Descriptive Bibliography of the Mormon Church*, vol. 1, *1830 to 1847* (Provo, UT: Religious Studies Center, 1997), 335.

14. Council of Fifty, Minutes, March 18, 1845, in *JSP*, CFM:328.

15. Council of Fifty, Minutes, March 22, 1845, in *JSP*, CFM:352.

16. Council of Fifty, Minutes, March 22, 1845, in *JSP*, CFM:354. A careful reading of the minutes downplays any assumed prophecy of Joseph Smith that the Saints would move to an interior valley of the Rocky Mountains.

17. Council of Fifty, Minutes, March 18, 1845, in *JSP*, CFM:329.

18. Gary S. Ford, "Cornelius P. Lott and His Contribution to the Temporal Salvation of the Latter-day Saint Pioneers through the Care of Livestock" (master's thesis, Brigham Young University, 2005), 105.

19. Letter from Orson Hyde, April 26, 1844, in *JSP*, CFM:184. This first report of Frémont was titled *Report on an Exploration of the Country Lying between the Missouri River and the Rocky Mountains, on the Line of the Kansas and Great Platte Rivers* (Washington: United States Senate, 1843).

20. "Capt. Frémont's Expedition," *Nauvoo Neighbor*, September 17, 1845, [1]; see Council of Fifty, Minutes, September 9, 1845, in *JSP*, CFM:472. For a fine recent study of Frémont's expedition and its impact on Latter-day Saint leaders, see Alexander L. Baugh, "John C. Frémont's 1843–44 Western Expedition and Its Influence on Mormon Settlement in Utah," *Utah Historical Quarterly* 83, no. 4 (Fall 2015): 254–69. Baugh argues that Frémont's study had "a profound influence on Brigham Young and the Church leadership and in their discussion to select the Wasatch region of northern Utah" as the main place for settlement. Baugh, "John C. Frémont's 1843–44 Western Expedition," 256.

21. Council of Fifty, Minutes, September 9, 1845, in *JSP*, CFM:472

22. Council of Fifty, Minutes, September 9, 1845, in *JSP*, CFM:475.

23. Council of Fifty, Minutes, January 11, 1846, in *JSP*, CFM:513–14.

24. Letter from Orson Hyde, April 26, 1844, in *JSP*, CFM:181–84.

25. Council of Fifty, Minutes, March 11, 1845, in *JSP*, CFM:299. The Western Mission was an assignment given to Jonathan Dunham and others in the spring of 1845 to gain permission from relocated Indian tribes living in the middle Missouri River region to establish settlements in the area and to obtain their pledge to assist the Saints in exploring the western countries. See Glen M. Leonard, *Nauvoo: A Place of Peace, a People of Promise* (Salt Lake City and Provo, Utah: Deseret Book and Brigham Young University Press, 2002), 514.

26. Council of Fifty, Minutes, January 11, 1846, in *JSP*, CFM:515, 517.

27. Council of Fifty, Minutes, January 11 and 13, 1846, in *JSP*, CFM:519, 525.

28. Council of Fifty, Minutes, January 13, 1846, in *JSP*, CFM:522–23. William Clayton recorded in his journal that on January 25 he met with the captains of the various companies to receive their final reports. *JSP*, CFM:550n32. The Saints began leaving Nauvoo just ten days later.

Chapter 14

THE COUNCIL OF FIFTY IN WESTERN HISTORY

Jedediah S. Rogers

In his Frontier Thesis, Frederick Jackson Turner postulated that social life in the West was a Darwinian sequence marked by "civil-savage encounter" and "free land." Humans who encountered the wilderness were at first at its mercy, until they slowly transformed it. As the wilderness receded and the "lines of civilization" advanced, settlement moved into a more developed stage.[1] Turner's thesis, written in 1893, drew from widely held nineteenth-century beliefs about the West and offered a compelling synthesis of American history that shaped history writing for generations. It also launched western American history as a distinct field. But Turner left out of his exposition individuals, groups, and ideas that we now consider to be quintessentially western, Mormons included.[2] After Turner, the field offered varying competing theories—each building on Turner's and past historiographical traditions—yet in each retelling, Mormons, with few exceptions, did not figure prominently. Although Mormons' own histories were Turnerian in some regards, the building of Zion by the communally oriented Latter-day Saints did not fit standard narratives of the West. Part of the blame may lie at the feet of western historians; Jan Shipps posits that western historians treat the West as a donut, with the conspicuous hole representing

Mormon country. Another metaphor, offered by the environmental and cultural historian Jared Farmer, draws on Great Basin geography: the provincialism of Utah history is like water that pools and never finds an outlet.[3]

Mormon studies has made inroads in the last few decades, garnering greater recognition and attention from academics and publics outside the Intermountain West. The Joseph Smith Papers Project is in part responsible for raising the stature and quality of Mormon history. And, coincidentally, its recently published volume of the Nauvoo minutes of the Council of Fifty can help us rethink not only the Mormon place in the West but the meaning of the Mormon experience to western history. Mormons had a unique but also distinctly American way of perceiving and approaching the Far West. Turner's compelling synthesis of American history, whatever its limitations, provides insight into the nineteenth-century Mormon mindset that viewed the interior West as a region without a history, a blank slate upon which they could imprint their mark.

. . .

The formation of the Council of Fifty in the spring of 1844 came just as Americans were widely awakening to the idea of a westward empire extending to the Pacific. Expanding the nation's borders satisfied America's divine mission, so the idea went. In his run for the US presidency, Joseph Smith blended the ideology of Democrats and Whigs; like ardent Democrats he looked westward and spoke of extending the nation, but in the Whig tradition he saw national influence as what the liberal minister William Ellery Channing called "a sublime moral empire, with a mission to diffuse freedom by manifesting its fruits, not to plunder, crush, and destroy."[4] The Great Emigration of 1842 and in following years gave the Americans a firm presence in Oregon Country, which after 1818 was jointly occupied by the British. Yet, as Richard White has observed, "The American nation that began to expand westward was neither militarily formidable nor a centralized state."[5]

Upon its formation, the Council of Fifty petitioned Congress for Smith to lead a company of one hundred thousand "armed volunteers" for protection along the emigrants' trails to Oregon and Texas.[6] Congress ignored the memorial, though in 1846 it did authorize establishing military posts along the road to Oregon and a regiment of mounted riflemen (part of a long tradition of federal government oversight and support of emigration and western settlement, which is ofttimes ignored in narratives of the western individualist). The council's military proposal was part of a larger western strategy that occupied the council through 1845: where to establish Mormon settlement beyond western Illinois. The council's project to expand outward no doubt drew from a national sense of Manifest Destiny. Smith and his associates, though, sought refuge from their enemies, and they seriously considered Oregon, Alta California, and the Republic of Texas as possibilities.[7]

The Council of Fifty unsuccessfully petitioned Congress to allow Joseph Smith to raise an army to protect American interests in the West. Daguerreotype of US Capitol by John Plumbe. Courtesy of Library of Congress, Washington, DC.

Geographically, Oregon had several advantages and may have appealed to Smith. Orson Hyde, writing from the nation's capital in 1844, apparently mailed Smith a prepublished copy of explorer John C. Frémont's report and identified the most attractive locations in Oregon as the "Umqua and Clamet Valleys."[8] As Frémont wrote, "Th[e] structure of the coast, backed by these two ranges of mountains [Cascades and Sierra Nevadas], with its concentration and unity of waters, gives to the country an immense military strength, and will probably render Oregon the most impregnable country in the world."[9] As appealing as Oregon appeared, however, Mormons clearly recognized that other Americans likewise coveted the region, particularly in Orson Hyde's view settlers from Missouri—"our old enemies, the mobocrats of Mo."[10] And it was not altogether clear that the United States would "win" Oregon or that it would be anything other than British. The council debated and even considered the "influence we can have under the British government," but discussion was brief; Brigham Young, who assumed chairmanship of the council after Smith's death, claimed to want "nothing to do with them."[11]

Mormons considered the government of the United States as intolerable to live under as that of Great Britain, if not more so. The minutes hint at disillusionment toward the US government. When the council drafted its own constitution, it mimicked the structure of the US Constitution and listed off grievances in the vein of the Declaration of Independence. As noted in the committee's constitution, the US government was beset, as were other governments, with "pride, corruption, impurity, intrigue, spiritual wickedness in high places, party spirit, faction, perplexity and distress of nations." The problem was not the principles undergirding the government but the absence of "the disposition and power to grant that protection to the persons and rights of man."[12] Members seemed to look forward to self-rule; George A. Smith said he "has long reflected that we ought to have a new government."[13] Their new home would be governed by their own laws, perhaps with creation of a territory through an act of Congress, as George Miller contemplated in correspondence with William P. Richards in 1845, or perhaps within domain of their own independent country.[14]

All this suggests, and the minutes seem to confirm, that Mormon leaders sought, at least initially, to shed the federal yoke and settle in a location outside of US jurisdiction. Smith spoke of "establish[ing] independent governments" from land carved from the Republic of Texas.[15] After Smith's death, Young remarked that "in the name of the Lord when we go from here, we will exalt the standard of liberty and make our own laws. When we go from here we dont calculate to go under any government but the government of God."[16] This intent to institute God's laws in many ways made Mormons distinct from other Americans who looked westward. William W. Phelps was prescient when he remarked in a council meeting in 1845 that "the greatest fears manifested by our enemies is the union of Church and State."[17]

Mormons cast their gaze westward to Alta or Upper California, then Mexican territory. From council deliberations, it seems Smith favored the Gulf of California as a location for his people; according to Erastus Snow, Smith always opposed settling away from the coast.[18] Young felt the same as late as mid-1845. In meeting after meeting, a member or the entire council expressed delight in a song composed by John Taylor, "The Upper California," expressing the intent to reside somewhere "Beside the great Pacific Sea."[19] Maps depicting Alta California as a large swath of land ranging from the Pacific to Colorado's Rocky Mountains give the sense that Upper California meant the Great Basin just as well as the Pacific coast. Descriptions in the council minutes clearly point to the virtues of settling close to the coast, however. Young's description of the ideal place for the Saints—"the advantages of Navigation and commerce," fortified between mountains, "gold and silver and precious stones," "raise all kinds of fruit," building and travel in ships, "where we can live without labor"— hardly fit the description of the Rocky Mountains.[20]

Not until late summer 1845 did leaders identify the Salt Lake Valley or possibly the Bear River Valley to the north as potential places to create a Mormon homeland. Knowledge of the Great Basin region came from trappers reporting to James Emmett, a council member, and from Frémont's 1845 publication of his Far West travels. The idea initially was that a Wasatch Range settlement would serve as an entrée to Mormon expansion to the Pacific and as a way station for weary travelers on the emigrants' trail.[21] The interior West did not have a coastline or favorable climate, but the geography and terrain had several advantages coveted by Mormon leadership. Young spoke of locating a place beyond the Rockies that could "easily be fortified against all hostile foes."[22] To another, the desert mountain terrain would mean they would "be free from the jealousies of any government." But the men also saw value in a landscape they did not know, opining for example that the mountains would shield them from cold and that near the West's "barren deserts" were "plains which are always rich and fertile."[23] Clearly, Young thought about desert lands not in the context that Mormons would come to see them—as land suited for a people determined to make it blossom as the rose—but as buffers from their enemies.

. . .

Not until they arrived in the Salt Lake Valley and got their hands dirty in the soil did they come to understand their new homeland. The Nauvoo minutes conclude in early 1846, but what we have from the available Council of Fifty record of the Mormons' first years in the Great Basin provides a dramatic juxtaposition between earlier perception and later realities.[24] This time the Mormons confronted a landscape that confounded and frightened them. What crops they planted were devoured by swarming crickets. Their cattle wallowed in deep snow with insufficient feed during the harsh winter of 1848 and 1849. Wild animals presented a threat to public safety and, in the case of wolves, a noise nuisance.

The story of the Latter-day Saints' first years in the West is one of desperation. It is also one of action: they sought to refashion their homeland as they imagined it. The Council of Fifty organized a public two-month hunt to eradicate wild animals, the result being an overwhelming slaughter.[25] It sent men to establish fisheries on Utah Lake, others to establish a tannery, still others to go east to buy sheep. The council outlawed the making of corn into whiskey, erected an armory, imposed taxes, redistributed money and food to those who had little, surveyed streets and fenced farm lots, constructed canals, located the site of the Salt Lake City cemetery, and reorganized the Nauvoo Legion. A committee superintended construction of fences in the "Big Field" to farm the land between 900 South and 2700 South. These efforts to build up not only the Great Salt Lake City but numerous other settlements came to characterize the idea, as expressed by the writer Wallace Stegner, that Mormons are more earthly, their communities more deeply rooted in the land than are other groups in the West.[26]

Stegner and other writers have rooted the Mormons to the western landscape; indeed, Mormon communities in a large swath of the American West—Mormon Country—appear as western as anything. Yet prior to their arrival in the Great Basin, Latter-day Saints were largely ignorant of the West and its peoples. When they did set their gaze west of the hundredth meridian, the land was unfamiliar and their perceptions often erroneous. Like other Americans, they looked to the West for opportunity, their aspirations part of a midcentury national project to spread beyond the nation's borders. The Mormons brought to that project their own style and agenda (in some respects counter to the mainstream) to shape the landscape according to their religious aspirations. Yet Mormon migration and settlement in the Great Basin has meant that the religious group originating in the frontier of western New York has become intricately intertwined with a national narrative that is western in its orientation and that the ambition to find a home that is unpeopled perfectly fits into the larger white western project to settle and reshape the West.

Mormons colonized the Far West with idealized views of the land that originated from their experience in the well-watered East and were refined by the religious assurances of a promised people. They envisioned not only a place where people could live, but a *well-ordered* place.[27] This idealized view—the quintessential pastoral landscape—possessed a redemptive quality that fit squarely with the nineteenth-century biblical view of land ordained by providence for "the use of man." Mormons brought with them religious beliefs about land and their role on it. They may have looked forward longingly to the millennial day when the high places would be made low and the crooked places straight, but they didn't have to wait. Their work was to realize that dream. They established the first modern irrigation system in the West and created an inland empire in the mountains that lasted nearly through the nineteenth century. It was a spiritual and temporal endeavor, and it gave meaning and vitality to the act of settlement and survival in this region.

Central to these ideas was the notion held by council members that Upper California, the Far West, and most particularly the eastern rim of the Great Basin constituted a region without a past, without a history. This was particularly important to a people driven out of several states at the behest of "old" settlers—in the words of George A. Smith in 1845, to "plant ourselves where there will be no one to say [we] are old settlers."[28] The Salt Lake Valley was for Young a blank canvas on which God could realize his handiwork: to organize a new society, to ensure that its citizens and the land conformed to the divine decree. Young reportedly told the council not to "suffer infernals, thieves, Murders, Whoremongers & every other wicked curse to [exist]," urging its members to blot out evildoing as prescribed by the body's very name, "The Kingdom of God and his Laws, with the keys and power thereof, and judgement in the hands of his servants."[29] Likewise, in council deliberations in early Utah we see this impulse to shape not just human behavior but the land in conformance with divine decree. Part of planting a new society in a new place was the idea of environmental transformation—the attempt to domesticate wild lands by subduing wild animals, for example.[30]

. . .

If the Mormon narrative sounds Turnerian, it is because in large measure it is—at least in the way that nineteenth-century Mormons spoke of their westward march of progress. Once ensconced in the valley of Salt Lake, Mormons represented their history as one of settling, even conquering, the wilderness. Speaking before his people on July 24, 1852, five years since the Mormons' arrival in the Great Basin, Young helped to create the mystique of the Mormons arriving in the mountain valleys and building a thriving city that "spread out from the east to the west, measurably so, but more extensively to the north and south."[31] George Q. Cannon, speaking before the Third National Irrigation Congress in 1894, said that when he first entered the Great Basin he "felt that there was a great future for" the western country. After describing the desolate conditions in the basin, Cannon looked back on what was accomplished with a great deal of pride, holding up the Mormon system of irrigation as a model for the other western territories and states.[32] Cannon's and other pioneer narratives underscored the God-ordained rightness of their cause, ignored other peoples or events that went counter to their retelling of the history, and emphasized the resulting environmental transformation of their civilizing work on the landscape.[33] The simplicity of the narrative—not unlike that of Turner—gave it staying power, even as it bolstered a rendering of the history that did not support its own weight. Yet however much the Frontier Thesis has since been discredited in the academy, Turnerian ideas live on prominently in the American imagination. His ideas would have reverberated with a late-nineteenth-century audience who could look back on the peopling of a continent with pride and nostalgia.

Whereas Turner spoke of the West as the westward march of human progress, a generation later Walter Webb, in his book *The Great Plains*, defined the West as a place. Webb borrowed from the ideas of John Wesley Powell to argue that the West's defining characteristic was a scarcity of water. Aridity forced westerners to innovate.[34] Some of this is reflected in the post-Nauvoo council record: the Mormon system of irrigation, the fencing of field to keep cattle from wandering, the extermination of predators. The communal energy of the Mormon project also helped mitigate terrestrial problems; for instance, Church-controlled irrigation differed from the more competitive orientation of prior appropriation practiced elsewhere.[35] The idea of water scarcity might help us reconsider the reasons for the council's vast State of Deseret: lack of rainfall and distance between water sources forced Young to explore large areas of land for expansion. Could it be that the expansive State of Deseret—the Mormon inland empire—was as much a product of environmental contingencies as geopolitical aspirations?

Taking a page from Webb, though considerably complicating his narrative, are the so-called New West historians, who identify the West as a particular region characterized by conflict and racial and ethnic diversity. The area bounded by the State of Deseret's original proposal is considered by historians as "unambiguous West," the core of what most historians think of as the West.[36] Other themes identified by New Western historians are reflected in the record of the council. Note, for instance, that historians have emphasized the community impulse of western settlement, not only of Mormons but of other groups in the region. Moreover, Mormon central planning, which eventually contributed to the success of dozens of western settlements, in some respects presaged the federal control that came to dominate the political, economic, and social fabric of the West.[37]

When I think about the Council of Fifty and its expansionist ideas for the West that never materialized, I look to another historiographical tradition represented most prominently by Henry Nash Smith's *Virgin Land* but also by many other western historians and writers since: the West as a state of mind, a myth, an identity.[38] As the Nauvoo minutes reveal, council members envisioned innumerable iterations of their planned western empire. The boundaries and contours remained opaque even as they attempted to bring geographical specificity to their discussions. The problem, of course, was that the territory of which they spoke was still relatively unknown and unpeopled—in some cases literal blank spaces on the map. Until they planted their feet on the soil, they could do little more than to envision and plan. Even after they arrived in the West, their aspirations remained just that. Their proposed State of Deseret never came to be, but it reflected the broader aspirations of Utah's first permanent Euro-American settlers, who dreamed and worked toward a Great Basin empire. Moreover, the idea of Mormon expansion had not reached a terminus. Settlements would continue to be made, and the imprint of the Mormon settler would continue to stamp itself on the land. The dream of a Mormon kingdom continued.

The American West has always been a place of dreams and aspirations. Few were as grand and idealistic as the Mormons. The Council of Fifty minutes provide a glimpse into the vision of a religious people who played an important role in western history—in the Mormon migration west, the Euro settlement of the Great Basin, and the political maneuverings for a Mormon state. It was a vision unique from the western experience, but it was also one that can be placed in western American historiography.

NOTES

1. Frederick Jackson Turner, "The Significance of the Frontier in American History" (paper presented at the American Historical Association conference, Chicago, July 12, 1893).

2. For the absence of Mormons in Turner's analysis, see Patricia Nelson Limerick, *Something in the Soil: Legacies and Reckonings in the New West* (New York: Norton, 2000), 239–40.

3. Jan Shipps, *Sojourner in the Promised Land: Forty Years among the Mormons* (Urbana: University of Illinois Press, 2000), 21; Jared Farmer, *On Zion's Mount: Mormons, Indians, and the American Landscape* (Cambridge, MA: Harvard University Press, 2008), 14.

4. Quoted in William Nester, *The Age of Jackson and the Art of American Power, 1815–1848* (Washington, DC: Potomac Books, 2013), 226.

5. Richard White, *It's Your Misfortune and None of My Own: A New History of the American West* (Norman: University of Oklahoma Press, 1991), 61.

6. Council of Fifty, Minutes, March 26, 1844, May 13, 1844, in Matthew J. Grow, Ronald K. Esplin, Mark Ashurst-McGee, Gerrit J. Dirkmaat, and Jeffrey D. Mahas, eds., *Council of Fifty, Minutes, March 1844–January 1846*, vol. 1 of the Administrative Records series of *The Joseph Smith Papers*, ed. Ronald K. Esplin, Matthew J. Grow, and Matthew C. Godfrey (Salt Lake City: Church Historian's Press, 2016), 62–73, 159–65 (hereafter *JSP*, CFM).

7. See, for example, Council of Fifty, Minutes, April 18, 1844, May 3, 1844, March 1, 1845, in *JSP*, CFM:115–16, 127–28, 137–47, 267–68. The council considered but soon abandoned Texas as a place to relocate en masse.

8. Letter from Orson Hyde, April 26, 1844, in *JSP*, CFM:181–84.

9. John C. Frémont, *Report of the Exploring Expedition to the Rocky Mountains in the Year 1842, and to Oregon and North California in the Years 1843–44* (Washington DC: Gales and Seaton, 1845), 275.

10. Letter from Orson Hyde, April 25, 1844, in *JSP*, CFM:177.

11. Council of Fifty, Minutes, April 11, 1845, in *JSP*, CFM:408.

12. Council of Fifty, Minutes, April 18, 1844, in *JSP*, CFM:111–12, 129.

13. Council of Fifty, Minutes, April 18, 1844, in *JSP*, CFM:116.

14. George Miller to William P. Richards, January 28, 1845, in *JSP*, CFM:240. Richards had suggested the idea of a "Mormon Reserve" to be created by an act of Congress.

15. Council of Fifty, Minutes, April 18, 1844, in *JSP*, CFM:127–28.

16. Council of Fifty, Minutes, March 1, 1845, in *JSP*, CFM:268; see also Young's remarks on January 11, 1846, in *JSP*, CFM:513.

17. Council of Fifty, Minutes, March 4, 1845, in *JSP*, CFM:285. This is not to say that Young did not calculate the possibility of Mexican territory becoming a US possession, and he almost certainly expected Alta California to come under the protective care of the United States. Seeking to curry favor from federal officials, Young informed President Polk in 1846 of Mormon plans to carve a state out of Upper California. Statehood would create "home-rule" within the American political system, even though it threatened to temper theocratic designs. Brigham Young to James K. Polk, August 9, 1846, Brigham Young Office Files, Church History Library, Salt Lake City, qtd. in Ronald W. Walker, "The Affair of the 'Runaway': Utah's First Encounter with the Federal Officers," *Journal of Mormon History* 39 (Fall 2013): 2.

18. Council of Fifty, Minutes, March 18 and 22, 1845, in *JSP*, CFM:328, 354.

19. See, for example, Council of Fifty, Minutes, April 11, 1845, in *JSP*, CFM:402–3.

20. Council of Fifty, Minutes, March 18, 1845, in *JSP*, CFM:328–29.

21. Council of Fifty, Minutes, September 9, 1845, in *JSP*, CFM:472.

22. Council of Fifty, Minutes, January 11, 1846, in *JSP*, CFM:513. Prior to Frémont, some mapmakers placed east-west ranges bounding the northern and southern boundaries of the Great Basin, suggesting an even more isolated and protected region.

23. Council of Fifty, Minutes, January 11, 1846, March 22, 1845, in *JSP*, CFM:515, 518, 352.

24. Prior to publication of the Nauvoo minutes of the Council of Fifty, what we knew about the Council of Fifty's role in the West derived from diaries, letters, and reminiscences of council members revealing either their impressions or their memories of council proceedings. These are compiled in my own edited volume, *The Council of Fifty: A Documentary History* (Salt Lake City: Signature Books, 2014). See also Klaus J. Hansen, *Quest for Empire: The Political Kingdom of God and the Council of Fifty in Mormon History* (East

Lansing: Michigan State University Press, 1967); D. Michael Quinn, "The Council of Fifty and Its Members, 1844 to 1945," *BYU Studies* 20 (Winter 1980): 163–97; and Andrew F. Ehat, "'It Seems Like Heaven Began on Earth': Joseph Smith and the Constitution of the Kingdom of God," *BYU Studies* 20 (Spring 1980): 253–80.

25. The council's war against "wasters and destroyers" is but one example of a broader tradition of categorizing and vilifying the animal kingdom. Like the land, animals fell into camps of "good" or "bad" depending on how they served humans. Patty Limerick has shown that in the West, so-called good animals had wildlife bureaus named for them—Fish and Game—while bad animals did not. See Patricia Nelson Limerick, *Legacy of Conquest: The Unbroken Past of the American West* (New York: Norton, 1987), 311–12. Wolves, mountain lions, and coyotes were often attacked by the government, as was the case with Utah's earliest Euro government in 1849. And the Council of Fifty's first laws in Utah, dated 1848, granting a bounty on wolf and other skins began a grand tradition in Utah of targeting animals deemed too wild, troublesome, or dangerous. See entries for the winter of 1848–49 and Historian's Office History, January 26, 1850, in Rogers, *Council of Fifty*.

26. Wallace Stegner, *Mormon Country,* ed. Erskine Caldwell, American Folkways series (New York: Duell, Sloan & Pearce, 1942).

27. Jedediah S. Rogers, *Roads in the Wilderness: Conflict in Canyon Country* (Salt Lake City: University of Utah Press, 2013), esp. chaps. 1 and 2.

28. Council of Fifty, Minutes, September 9, 1845, in *JSP*, CFM:476.

29. John D. Lee, Diary, March 3, 1849, in Rogers, *Council of Fifty*, 161. For the council's name, see Council of Fifty, Minutes, March 14, 1844, in *JSP*, CFM:48; see also William Clayton, Journal, January 1, 1845, in Rogers, *Council of Fifty*, 29.

30. See Rogers, *Council of Fifty*, esp. entries for 1848 and 1849.

31. Brigham Young, July 24, 1852, in *Journal of Discourses* (Liverpool: F. D. Richards, 1855), 1:146.

32. George Q. Cannon, "The Mormon Land System in Utah," *Irrigation Age: A Journal of Western America* 7 (July 1894): 188–89.

33. The Mormons' narrative that they had transformed the environment is taken up in Farmer, *On Zion's Mount*, 105–38; and Jon T. Coleman, *Vicious: Wolves and Men in America* (New Haven, CT: Yale University Press, 2004), 173–87.

34. Walter Webb, *The Great Plains* (1931; repr., Lincoln: University of Nebraska Press, 1981).

35. See John Bennion, "Water Law on the Eve of Statehood: Israel Bennion and a Conflict in Vernon, 1893–1896," *Utah Historical Quarterly* 82 (Fall 2014): 289–305.

36. Walter Nugent, "Where Is the American West: Report on a Survey," *Montana: The Magazine of Western History* 42 (Spring 1992): 2–23.

37. For works on the federal presence, see Karen R. Merrill, *Public Lands and Political Meaning: Ranchers, the Government, and the Property between Them* (Berkeley: University of California Press, 2002); and Leisl Carr Childers, *The Size of the Risk: Histories of Multiple Use in the Great Basin* (Norman: University of Oklahoma Press, 2015).

38. Henry Nash Smith, *Virgin Land: The American West as Symbol and Myth* (Cambridge, MA: Harvard University Press, 1950).

Chapter 15

THE COUNCIL OF FIFTY AND THE SEARCH FOR RELIGIOUS LIBERTY

W. Paul Reeve

On July 22, 2014, I received a brief email from Peggy Fletcher Stack, the award-winning religion reporter at the *Salt Lake Tribune*: "Paul, I am doing a short piece on Mormon pioneers for Thursday. Would you be willing to send me three surprising or intriguing facts about the pioneers and the trek that most people don't know? I don't need anything lengthy, just a paragraph on each."

In response, I sent Peggy the following paragraph:

> Considering the way in which some Pioneer Day talks in Mormon congregations sometimes conflate American patriotism with the Mormon arrival in the Salt Lake Valley, it seems evident that most Mormons today don't realize the depth of mistrust and resentment some Mormon pioneers harbored toward the United States in 1846 and 1847. When the Mormons arrived in the Great Basin, they were actually arriving in northern Mexico. They crossed an international border and were fleeing the United States. The U.S. war with Mexico was ongoing. When some Mormons first learned of that war, they hoped Mexico would win. Pioneer Hosea Stout, for example, wrote in his diary, "I confess that I was glad to learn of war

against the United States and was in hopes that it might never end untill they were entirely destroyed for they had driven us into the wilderness & was now laughing at our calamities."[1]

After Stack's story appeared in print and was subsequently passed around on Facebook, a bit of a dustup ensued.[2] A few people on Facebook wanted me to know that their Mormon pioneer ancestors were loyal Americans and that I had done them a disservice in the way that I had characterized the mistrust and resentment that some pioneers harbored toward the United States. After now having read the Council of Fifty minutes, if I had to answer Stack's request today, I would suggest that my original answer, if anything, *understated* the mistrust and resentment some Mormons bore toward the United States. I would amplify the degree and depth of mistrust—and even outright rejection—of the United States and its Constitution that animated the Council of Fifty's attitude.

A PREVIOUSLY GLOSSED-OVER PERIOD

In terms of an overall assessment of the council minutes, let me state that while some students of the Mormon past might be disappointed in the Council of Fifty minutes because they do not contain salacious evidence that might bring Mormonism to its knees, what I found was engaging and even sometimes riveting. It was as if I had a front-row seat as I watched the tragic unraveling of the Mormon community at Nauvoo. The time period covered in the minutes is significant. The two years from 1844 to 1846 seem so crucial, yet they fall between the cracks in terms of how historians have typically told the Mormon story.

Traditionally, historians end their discussion of the early era of Mormonism with Joseph Smith's murder in June 1844 and then begin a discussion of the Great Basin era with Brigham Young's departure from Nauvoo in February 1846 or Young's arrival in the Salt Lake Valley in July 1847. If for no other reason, the Council of Fifty volume is essential for its fascinating and insightful lens—from an administrative perspective— into the two years that historians of the Mormon past typically only gloss over or ignore altogether. The unease and ongoing tension with old

Nauvoo, Illinois, 1846. Glass plate negative made by Charles W. Carter of original daguerreotype by Lucian R. Foster. Courtesy of Church History Library, Salt Lake City.

settlers in Hancock County sometimes drip from the pages as does the Latter-day Saint leadership's efforts at finding a new place of refuge for the Saints. If readers are able to set aside their knowledge of how the story plays out and immerse themselves in the minds of council members who were not privy to that knowledge, the bleakness and even desperation of the Saints' precarious situation from 1844 to 1846 is powerfully embodied in these minutes.

RESENTMENT AND ANGER TOWARD US GOVERNMENT

I felt the depth of council members' despair over a continued inability to find judicial, executive, or legislative justice for the wrongs they had endured, including the murder of their leaders Hyrum and Joseph Smith. I was reminded of Alexis de Tocqueville's assessment of one of the inherent weaknesses he found in American democracy, something he called the tyranny of the majority:

> What I most criticize about democratic government as it has been organized in the United States, is not its weaknesses as many people in Europe claim, but on the contrary, its irresistible strength. And what repels me the most in America is not the extreme liberty that reigns there; it is the slight guarantee against tyranny that is found.
>
> When a man or a party suffers from an injustice in the United States, to whom do you want them to appeal? To public opinion? That is what forms the majority. To the legislative body? It represents the majority and blindly obeys it. To the executive power? It is named by the majority and serves it as a passive instrument. To the police? The police are nothing other than the majority under arms. To the jury? The jury is the majority vested with the right to deliver judgments. The judges themselves, in certain states, are elected by the majority. However iniquitous or unreasonable the measure that strikes you may be, you must therefore submit to it or flee. What is that if not the very soul of tyranny under the forms of liberty?[3]

The Council of Fifty minutes made Tocqueville's point real to me in a way that academic histories of Mormonism have not been able to do. Joseph Smith was especially concerned that the US Constitution did not protect minority rights. "There is only two or three things lacking in the constitution of the United States," Smith contended, and it was the guarantee of rights and freedom for all, regardless of religious affiliation. He was dismayed that the federal government refused to intervene on behalf of Mormon property rights and religious liberty in Missouri. He wished that the Constitution required "the armies of the government" to enforce "principles of liberty" for all people, not merely the Protestant majority. He advocated severe penalties for a "President or Governor who does not do this," suggesting that "he shall lose his head" or that "when a Governor or president will not protect his subjects he ought to be put away from his office."[4] The failure of state or federal governments to address Mormon grievances clearly bothered Smith and was a prime motivator in his appointing a committee from among the council to draft a new constitution. That the committee's efforts failed to produce a viable document testifies to the difficulties of constitution writing in general and to the challenges of writing specific guarantees against oppression toward marginalized groups. That a committee attempted such a feat affirms the depth of despair Mormon leaders felt at their status as a religious minority and the gravity of their perception that the US Constitution had failed them.

Joseph Smith compensated for the lack of liberty he saw in the US Constitution with an expansive vision of religious freedom at Nauvoo and for his proposed kingdom of God on earth. He included as members in the Council of Fifty those of other faiths or of no faith as an explicit demonstration of his views. He stated on April 11, 1844, that there were men (three total) admitted to the council who were not Latter-day Saints and who "neither profess any creed or religious sentiment whatever." They were admitted to the council, in part, to demonstrate that "in the organization of this kingdom men are not consulted as to their religious opinions or notions in any shape or form whatever and that we act upon the broad and liberal principal that all men have equal rights, and ought to be respected, and that every man has a privilege in this organization of choosing for himself voluntarily his God, and what he pleases for his religion."[5]

For Joseph Smith, it was not enough to merely tolerate people of other faiths or of no faith. Religious bigotry had no place in his worldview. He stated, "God cannot save or damn a man only on the principle that every man acts, chooses and worships for himself; hence the importance of thrusting from us every spirit of bigotry and intolerance towards a mans religious sentiments, that spirit which has drenched the earth with blood." He called the council to witness that "the principles of intollerance and bigotry never had a place in this kingdom, nor in my breast, and that he is even then ready to die rather than yeild to such things. Nothing can reclaim the human mind from its ignorance, bigotry, superstition &c," he insisted, "but those grand and sublime principles of equal rights and universal freedom to all men."[6] Joseph Smith and other members of the council came to believe that the US Constitution had failed the Latter-day Saints on this count—that their rights had not been protected. Thus they needed to draft a new constitution to rectify this inadequacy.

DEVOTION TO THE NATION

Despite the substantial resentment manifested in the Council of Fifty minutes toward the United States and its Constitution, council members also demonstrated an ongoing devotion to the nation. Considerable paradox is thus bound up in the minutes and in the hearts of its members. Under Joseph Smith's leadership, the council "agreed to look to some place where we can go and establish a Theocracy either in Texas or Oregon or somewhere in California."[7] Council members also "spoke very warmly" about "forming a constitution which shall be according to the mind of God and erect it between the heavens and the earth where all nations might flow unto it."[8] At the same time, the council petitioned the US Congress to authorize Joseph Smith to "raise a company of one hundred thousand armed volunteers" to protect and facilitate US western expansion. Such a plan, the council suggested, would demonstrate Joseph Smith's "loyalty to our confederate Union, and the constitution of our Republic."[9] Joseph Smith also ran for president of the United States, and council members left Nauvoo on electioneering missions. Under Brigham Young's leadership, council members talked about declaring themselves an independent nation even as the council drafted letters to every governor of every state in the nation asking if each governor might be willing to accept Latter-day Saints as a group of religious refugees in his respective state. Only the governor of Arkansas, Thomas S. Drew, wrote to Young in response. Drew claimed that he was unable to help and that the Mormons would be better off with their proposed move west.[10]

Perhaps these paradoxes foreground the tension that US Mormons continue to exhibit in the twenty-first century, with their desire to both belong and to be distinct. Perhaps that desire is a holdover from a much more fraught historical climate in the mid-to-late 1840s that ultimately propelled Mormons outside of the United States altogether and then put them at odds with the American nation for the rest of the century. As William W. Phelps said in one council meeting, he was in favor of "letting the United States and the British governments alone, we are better without them."[11] It was a sentiment that continued to animate Mormon interactions with the nation on occasion. By the early twentieth century, Mormon leaders were ready to move toward accommodation, yet an underlying wariness still sometimes stirred both sides.

THE WEST

My final impression from reading the minutes highlights the power that the American West (or what would become the American West) had over the imaginations of members of the Council of Fifty. The council's very organization centered on the idea that Mormons needed to find a new location for Mormon settlement (initially, the search was for an additional location for Mormons—another gathering place not to replace Nauvoo but to supplement it, with some early discussion and efforts focused on Texas as a place where Mormons with slaves might gather to avoid the problems that moving to a northern state might present for slaveholding converts). Oregon and California were also places that captured the council's imagination.

The historian Frederick Jackson Turner talked about the West as a safety valve—a location that allowed the crowded cities and factories of the East to release the pressure of America's growing industrialization by offering free land and a new destiny in the West.[12] The Council of Fifty viewed the West as a safety valve of its own making. What council members sought to flee was not the growing squalor of industrial centers but a government that failed to protect minority rights. The West of their imagination was a place outside the bounds of firm state control, and for those reasons they zeroed in on Oregon, Texas, and Alta, or Upper, California. Over the chronological course of the minutes, council members for various reasons became less enthused about Texas and Oregon and more focused on California (an expansive geographic term at the time that encompassed the northern Mexican frontier, including the Great Basin). "The sooner we are where we can plant ourselves where there will be no one to say [that] they are [the] old settlers the better," George A. Smith said on September 9, 1845.[13] At that same meeting, Brigham Young stated that "it has been proved that there is not much difficulty in sending people beyond the mountains. We have designed sending them somewhere near the Great Salt Lake."[14]

Historians have long known of the advanced preparations of the Mormons for their removal west, especially their foreknowledge of the resources that the West had to offer and of the potential sites for a future relocation.[15] The Council of Fifty minutes add detail and a more concrete timeline to that knowledge. As early as September 1845, Young had zeroed in on the Great Salt Lake. Sometimes, stories that circulate in popular Mormon culture suggest that the Saints were driven from their homes in Illinois and wandered aimlessly westward, not knowing their destination until, on July 24, 1847, Brigham Young declared that the Salt Lake Valley was "the right place." Young, in fact, arrived two days after the initial Mormon migrants entered the valley on July 22. He joined that vanguard group on July 24 at their camp between present-day Third and Fourth South and Main and State Streets, where the beginnings of the initial Mormon settlement were already under way. Young's declarative statement that day was thus a confirmation of a decision already made, something Young had contemplated with the Council of Fifty as early as the fall of 1845.[16]

Council members were also purposefully looking for a place outside of firm governmental control for their settlement, and northern Mexico fit that bill. They were fully aware that they were leaving the United States and crossing an international border. Mexico's lack of direct dominion over its northern frontier was what made it so desirable to the Saints. Erastus Snow observed on March 22, 1845, that "the only difficulty there appears to be in the way of our locating in California is the Mexican government, and he has no fears about them. . . . He knows the Mexican government is weak, and they have never taken measures to place themselves in a situation of defence: They are too weak to maintain themselves against their own enemies in their midst. Every information he has been able to get goes to satisfy him that there is a mere form of government but not much power."[17] As Snow viewed it, the Great Basin existed in a power vacuum, which made it an attractive destination for the Saints, who were looking for a place to establish a religious kingdom without the same type of outside interference that had worked to their disadvantage in Missouri and Illinois.

CONCLUSION

The Council of Fifty minutes, in summary, offer an important administrative perspective into a crucial two years in Mormon history. They highlight the mounting tension between the Saints and the American nation and offer a much longer view of events leading up to the Utah War of 1857–58. Future histories of that war will need to account for the attitudes and perspectives toward the federal government brewing among Mormon leaders in the 1840s as the beginnings of a fracturing relationship that continued to deteriorate through the 1850s. These insights and many more will give students of Mormon history much to contemplate as they pore over the Council of Fifty minutes in search of new understanding.

NOTES

1. Juanita Brooks, ed., *On the Mormon Frontier: The Diary of Hosea Stout, 1844–1861*, 2 vols. (Salt Lake City: University of Utah Press, 1964), 1:163–64; see also John F. Yurtinus, "'Here Is One Man Who Will Not Go, Dam'um': Recruiting the Mormon Battalion in Iowa Territory," *BYU Studies* 21, no. 4 (Fall 1981): 475–87.

2. Peggy Fletcher Stack, "This Is the Place for Facts You Might Not Know about Mormon Pioneers," *Salt Lake Tribune*, July 24, 2014, http://www.sltrib.com /sltrib/news/58216230-78/mormon-pioneers-mormons-companies.html.csp.

3. Alexis de Tocqueville, *Democracy in America: Historical-Critical Edition of De la démocratie en Amérique*, ed. Eduardo Nolla, trans. James T. Schleifer (Indianapolis: Liberty Fund, 2010), 2:413–14.

4. Council of Fifty, Minutes, April 11, 1844, in Matthew J. Grow, Ronald K. Esplin, Mark Ashurst-McGee, Gerrit J. Dirkmaat, and Jeffrey D. Mahas, eds., *Council of Fifty, Minutes, March 1844–January 1846*, vol. 1 of the Administrative Records series of *The Joseph Smith Papers*, ed. Ronald K. Esplin, Matthew J. Grow, and Matthew C. Godfrey (Salt Lake City: Church Historian's Press, 2016), 101, (hereafter *JSP*, CFM).

5. Council of Fifty, Minutes, April 11, 1844, in *JSP*, CFM:97.

6. Council of Fifty, Minutes, April 11, 1844, in *JSP*, CFM:97, 100.

7. Council of Fifty, Minutes, March 11, 1844, in *JSP*, CFM:40.

8. Council of Fifty, Minutes, March 11, 1844, in *JSP*, CFM:42.

9. Council of Fifty, Minutes, March 26, 1844, in *JSP*, CFM:68, 69.

10. *JSP*, CFM:389.

11. Council of Fifty, Minutes, April 11, 1845, in *JSP*, CFM:409.

12. George Rogers Taylor, *The Turner Thesis Concerning the Role of the Frontier in American History*, rev. ed., Heath New History Series (Boston: Heath, 1956).

13. Council of Fifty, Minutes, September 9, 1845, in *JSP*, CFM:476.

14. Council of Fifty, Minutes, September 9, 1845, in *JSP*, CFM:472.

15. Lewis Clark Christian, "Mormon Foreknowledge of the West," *BYU Studies* 21, no. 4 (Fall 1981): 403–15.

16. W. Randall Dixon, "From Emigration Canyon to City Creek: Pioneer Trail and Campsites in the Salt Lake Valley in 1847," *Utah Historical Quarterly* 65 (Spring 1997): 155–64.

17. Council of Fifty, Minutes, March 22, 1845, in *JSP*, CFM:354.

CONTRIBUTORS

Richard E. Bennett is a professor of Church history and doctrine at Brigham Young University. His publications include *We'll Find the Place: The Mormon Exodus, 1846–1848* (1997) and *Mormons at the Missouri, 1846–1852: "And Should We Die . . ."* (1987).

Christopher James Blythe is a historian with the Joseph Smith Papers Project. His published work has appeared in journals such as *Journal of Mormon History*, *BYU Studies Quarterly*, *Nova Religio*, and *Material Religion*.

Marilyn Bradford is a research assistant at the Church History Department, The Church of Jesus Christ of Latter-day Saints. She graduated with a degree in history from the University of California, Berkeley in 2015 and will be pursuing a master's in history education.

Richard Lyman Bushman is Gouverneur Morris Professor Emeritus of History, Columbia University, and former Howard W. Hunter Chair of Mormon Studies at Claremont Graduate University. He is a member of the National Advisory Board and a former general editor of the Joseph Smith Papers Project.

Gerrit J. Dirkmaat, an assistant professor of Church history and doctrine at Brigham Young University, has coedited several volumes of *The Joseph Smith Papers*, including *Council of Fifty, Minutes: March 1844–January 1846* (2016). He is coauthor of *From Darkness unto Light: Joseph Smith's Translation and Publication of the Book of Mormon* (2015).

Matthew C. Godfrey is a general editor and the managing historian of the Joseph Smith Papers Project. He is the former president of Historical Research Associates, a historical and archeological consulting firm, and is the author of *Religion, Politics, and Sugar: The Mormon Church, the Federal Government, and the Utah-Idaho Sugar Company, 1907–1921* (2007).

Matthew J. Grow, director of publications for the LDS Church History Department, is a historian specializing in Mormon history. Grow coauthored a biography of Parley P. Pratt with Terryl Givens. He formerly directed the Center for Communal Studies housed at the University of Southern Indiana.

Jeffrey D. Mahas coedited *Council of Fifty, Minutes: March 1844–January 1846* (2016). He is a documentary editor with the Joseph Smith Papers Project and is pursuing a PhD in history from the University of Utah.

Patrick Q. Mason is Howard W. Hunter Chair of Mormon Studies and dean of the School of Arts and Humanities at Claremont Graduate University and a nationally recognized authority on Mormonism. His publications include *The Mormon Menace: Violence and Anti-Mormonism in the Postbellum South* (2011), *Planted: Belief and Belonging in an Age of Doubt* (2015), and *What Is Mormonism? A Student's Introduction* (2017).

Spencer W. McBride is a historian whose research interests include the intersections of religion and politics in early America. He is a volume editor with the Joseph Smith Papers Project and the author of *Pulpit and Nation: Clergymen and the Politics of Revolutionary America* (2016).

Nathan B. Oman is Rollins Professor of Law at William & Mary Law School. His legal scholarship has focused on the philosophy of contract law and on Mormon legal history.

Benjamin E. Park is an assistant professor of history at Sam Houston State University. His first book, *American Nationalisms: Imagining Union in an Age of Revolutions,* is forthcoming from Cambridge University Press in 2018.

W. Paul Reeve is a professor of history and the director of graduate studies in history at the University of Utah. He is the author of *Religion of a Different Color: Race and the Mormon Struggle for Whiteness* (2015).

Jedediah S. Rogers is co-managing editor of the *Utah Historical Quarterly* and a senior historian, Utah Division of State History. His publications include *The Council of Fifty: A Documentary History* (2014).

R. Eric Smith is the editorial manager for the Publications Division, Church History Department, The Church of Jesus Christ of Latter-day Saints. In that role, he edits print and web publications for the Church Historian's Press, including publications of the Joseph Smith Papers Project. He previously was an editor for the church's Curriculum Department, and before that he practiced law for a Salt Lake City firm.

Richard E. Turley Jr. is the managing director of the Public Affairs Department, The Church of Jesus Christ of Latter-day Saints. He was previously an Assistant Church Historian and Recorder and the managing director of the Church History Department.

ACKNOWLEDGMENTS

We appreciate the Religious Studies Center staff for their assistance through the peer review, design, editing, and marketing. Thomas A. Wayment and Joany O. Pinegar shepherded the book through the peer-review process. Brent R. Nordgren and Madison Swapp edited photos and designed the book. R. Devan Jensen, Tyler Balli, Mandi Diaz, Shannon K. Taylor, Kimball Gardner, and Leah Emal edited the chapters. Erin Gazdik helped with the promotional materials.

INDEX